THE COMPLETE BOOK OF CROSS STITCH

Jane Alford   Angela Beazley   Gail Bussi
Dorothea Hall   Julie Hasler   Susie Johns
Christina Marsh   Shirley Watts

MEREHURST

THE CHARTS

Some of the designs in this book are very detailed and due to
inevitable space limitations, the charts may be shown on a
comparatively small scale; in such cases, readers may find it
helpful to have the particular chart with which they are
currently working enlarged.

THREADS

The projects in this book were all stitched with DMC, Anchor or
Madeira stranded cotton embroidery threads. The keys given with each
chart list thread combinations for all three types of thread.
It should be pointed out that the shades produced by different
companies vary slightly, and it is not always possible to find
identical colours in a different range.
Due to the difficulty of true photographic colour reproduction, the
threads recommended do not always match the photographs exactly.

Published in 1996 by Merehurst Limited
Ferry House, 51-57 Lacy Road, Putney, London SW15 1PR

Text pp18-21, 46-9, 92-3, 102-5, 114-17, 128-9 and 154-7 © Copyright 1995 Jane Alford
Text pp22-9, 36-7 and 50-53 © Copyright 1995 Gail Bussi
Text pp144-5, 150-53, 158-61, 172-89, 194-7 and 202-17 © Copyright 1995 Julie Hasler
Text pp54-7, 98-101 and 110-13 © Copyright 1995 Shirley Watts
All other text © Copyright 1995 Merehurst Limited
Photography and illustrations © Copyright 1995 Merehurst Limited
ISBN 1 85391 553 X

A catalogue record for this book is available from the British Library.

Edited by Heather Dewhurst and Diana Lodge
Designed by Maggie Aldred and Kit Johnson
Photography by Marie-Louise Avery (all pages except pp14-19, 46-7, 82-3, 90-91,
126-7, 154-5 and 170-87); Di Lewis (pp14-15); and Debbie Patterson (pp18-19,
46-7, 82-3, 90-91, 126-7, 154-5 and 170-87)
Illustrations by John Hutchinson
Typesetting by Dacorum Type & Print, Hemel Hempstead
Colour separation by Fotographics Limited, UK – Hong Kong
Printed in Singapore by Toppan Printing Co.

*Merehurst is the leading publisher of craft books and has an excellent range
of titles to suit all levels. Please send to the address above for our
free catalogue, stating the title of this book.*

CONTENTS

INTRODUCTION

The immense popularity of cross stitch embroidery, with its distinctive range of decorative effects, can be seen in the growing interest for hand-embroidered gifts and items for the home. This book has something for everyone as it is filled with a huge variety of cross stitch projects covering many favourite stitching themes: flowers, cottages, gardens, animals, teddies, romantic occasions and, not least, Christmas. The wide range of projects, which cater for both the cross stitch novice and the seasoned stitcher, include cushions, pictures, greetings cards, samplers, coasters and photograph frames.

'Bless This House', the first section in the book, takes the home as its theme and includes several charming pictures, samplers and trinket boxes featuring cosy cottages, the symbol of security, friendliness and tradition the whole world over. The section entitled 'Glorious Gardens' is a celebration of gardens everywhere, from neat and formal town patios, bijou gardens in the suburbs, and grand estates in the country, to pretty, rambling cottage gardens. We all have a favourite flower, and hopefully some of them have been included in this floral collection.

'Fruits of Nature' should appeal to everyone's tastebuds, with a fruity cushion, a strawberry garland table set, fruity pictures and even a set of matching citrus tea towels designed to bring added zest to your washing up! Flowers are subjects that are perennial favourites and not least for stitching. The section 'Fabulous Flowers' incorporates a set of designs with flowers as its theme, including roses, foxgloves, pansies and numerous others. In this section you can choose from samplers, a wall-hanging, pictures and photo frames and an array of delightful small gifts.

'Romantic Moments' is a section devoted especially to that most romantic of occasions – the wedding. You can make a pretty personalized sampler, or choose from an array of special gifts to make for your loved ones on this special day. Animals provide another popular subject among stitchers, both old and young. The section 'Animal Friends' offers delightful ideas for stitching a

knitting bag featuring naughty kittens, an animal alphabet for personalizing clothes, bags and even cushions, as well as a colourful butterfly sampler. Following on from this theme, the section entitled 'Teddies to Treasure' includes a host of amusing teddy bear projects, ranging from greetings cards and cushions to a baby's coverlet and toy bag for the nursery, all of which feature those irresistably cuddly teddy bears.

Finally, you can celebrate Christmas in cross stitch with a whole range of festive stitching treats. For novices, what could be easier than stitching Christmas cards for your family and friends, while for the more experienced stitchers, there are Christmas crackers, a Christmas stocking, snowflake glass coasters, and festive table linen, to name but a few of the exciting and challenging projects included.

Cross stitch is a wonderfully easy stitch to learn and you do not require years of experience to produce very pleasing results. Each design is carefully charted and colour coded and is accompanied by simple step-by-step instructions for making up the item.

Even if you have never done cross stitch before, this book will enable you to master all the techniques you need to know. The most inexperienced stitcher will be surprised and delighted with the results they achieve, although it is sensible to choose a reasonably simple project for your first attempt. While some designs are very easy and quite suitable for beginners, others are a little more challenging and may involve working with many colours. Handling them can seem daunting at first, but your skill will very quickly improve with practice. Learning to work with several needles threaded with different colours is useful, and you will avoid having to start and finish new threads with each colour area.

There is also a Basic Skills section, which covers everything from preparing and stretching your fabric in an embroidery frame, learning the stitches you will need to use, to mounting your cross stitch ready for display. There are clear and simple illustrations to help you with all the stitches you will need for every project in this book. All the necessary skills are simply explained, thus ensuring that, whatever your level of experience, you will be able to enjoy creating beautiful things for you, your friends and your family.

Happy Stitching!

BASIC SKILLS

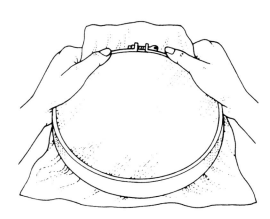

BEFORE YOU BEGIN

PREPARING THE FABRIC

Even with an average amount of handling, many evenweave fabrics tend to fray at the edges, so it is a good idea to overcast the raw edges, using ordinary sewing thread, before you begin. Alternatively, wrap masking tape over the edges.

FABRIC

Some projects in this book use Aida fabric, which is ideal both for beginners and more advanced stitchers as it has a surface of clearly designated squares. All Aida fabric has a count, which refers to the number of squares (each stitch covers one square) to 2.5cm (1in); the higher the count, the smaller the finished stitching.

Other projects in this book use either 14- or 18-count Aida, popular and readily available sizes, in a wide variety of colours. Linen has been used for several projects in this book; although less simple to stitch on than Aida fabric (because you need to count over a specified number of threads) it does give a very attractive, traditional finish. The most commonly available linen has 28 threads to 2.5cm (1in), which when worked over two threads gives a stitch count of 14 to 2.5cm (1in).

THE INSTRUCTIONS

Each project begins with a full list of the materials that you will require. Aida, Tula, Lugana and Linda are all fabrics produced by Zweigart. Note that the measurements given for the embroidery fabric include a minimum of 3cm (1¼in) all around to allow for stretching it in a frame and preparing the edges to prevent them from fraying.

Colour keys for stranded embroidery cottons – DMC, Anchor or Madeira – are given with each chart. It is assumed that you will need to buy one skein of each colour mentioned in a particular key, even though you may use less, but where two or more skeins are needed, this information is included in the main list of requirements.

To work from the charts, particularly those where several symbols are used in close proximity, some readers may find it helpful to have the chart enlarged so that the squares and symbols can be seen more easily. Many photocopying services will do this for a minimum charge.

Before you begin to embroider, always mark the centre of the design with two lines of basting stitches, one vertical and one horizontal, running from edge to edge of the fabric, as indicated by the arrows on the charts.

As you are stitching, use the centre lines given on the chart and the basting threads on your fabric as reference points for counting the squares and threads so that you can position your design accurately on the fabric.

WORKING IN A HOOP

A hoop is the most popular frame for use with small areas of embroidery. It consists of two rings, one fitted inside the other; the outer ring usually has an adjustable screw attachment so that it can be tightened to hold the stretched fabric in place. Embroidery hoops are readily available in several sizes, ranging from 10cm (4in) in diameter to quilting hoops with a diameter of 38cm (15in). Hoops with table stands or floor stands attached are also available.

1 To stretch your fabric in a hoop, place the area to be embroidered over the inner ring and press the outer ring over it, with the tension screw released. Tissue paper can be placed between the outer ring and the embroidery, so that the hoop does not mark the fabric. Lay the tissue paper over the fabric when you set it in the hoop, then tear away the central embroidery area. If the fabric creases, release the outer loop and try again.

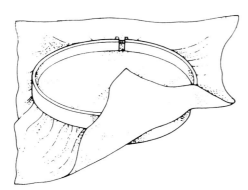

2 Smooth the fabric and, if necessary, straighten the grain before tightening the screw. The fabric should be evenly stretched.

EXTENDING EMBROIDERY FABRIC

It is easy to extend a piece of embroidery fabric, such as a bookmark, to stretch it in a hoop.

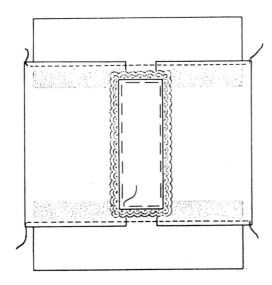

● Fabric oddments of a similar weight can be used. Simply cut four pieces to size (in other words, to the measurement that will fit both the embroidery fabric and your hoop) and baste them to each side of the embroidery fabric before stretching it in the hoop in the usual way.

WORKING IN A RECTANGULAR FRAME

Rectangular frames are more suitable for larger pieces of embroidery. They consist of two rollers, with tapes attached, and two flat side pieces, which slot into the rollers and are held in place by pegs or screw attachments. Available in different sizes, frames are measured by the length of the roller tape, ranging from 30cm (12in) to 68cm (27in).

10

As alternatives to a slate frame, canvas stretchers and the backs of old picture frames can be used. Provided there is sufficient extra fabric around the finished size of the embroidery, the edges of the fabric can be turned under and simply attached to the sides of the frame with drawing pins (thumb tacks) or staples.

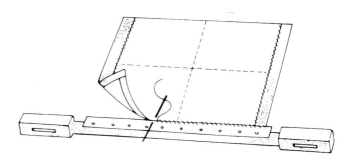

1 To stretch your fabric in a rectangular frame, cut out the fabric, allowing at least an extra 5cm (2in) all around the finished size of the embroidery. Baste a single 12mm (½in) turning on the top and bottom edges and oversew strong tape, 2.5cm (1in) wide, to the other two sides. Mark the centre line on the fabric both ways with large basting stitches. Working from the centre outwards and using a needle and strong thread, oversew the top and bottom edges to the roller tapes. Fit the side pieces into the slots, and roll any extra fabric on one roller until the fabric is completely taut.

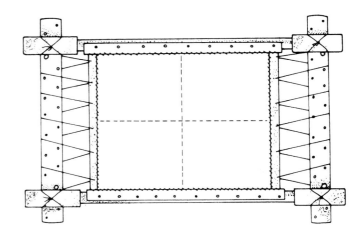

2 Insert the pegs or adjust the screw attachments to secure the frame. Thread a large-eyed needle (chenille needle) with strong thread or fine string and lace both edges of the fabric, securing the ends around the intersections of the frame. Lace the webbing at 2.5cm (1in) intervals, stretching the fabric evenly.

WORKING WITH WASTE CANVAS

Waste canvas has been used for some of the designs in this book. This canvas, quite simply, provides a removable grid over which you can stitch on unevenly-woven fabrics. Once the design has been stitched, the canvas is removed. Firstly, determine the size of the design, and cut a piece of canvas that allows a border of at least 5cm (2in) all around. Baste the waste canvas to the design area of the fabric/item you are using. Stitch your design in the usual way, making sure it is centred on the fabric/item. When stitching is complete, remove the basting stitches and lightly dampen the canvas with water. Slowly and gently pull out the threads of canvas, one at a time, using a pair of tweezers. Don't hurry this process, as it could result in spoiling your stitching. You may need to re-dampen stubborn threads that will not pull out.

THE STITCHES

CROSS STITCH

For all cross stitch embroidery, the following two methods of working are used. In each case, neat rows of vertical stitches are produced on the back of the fabric.

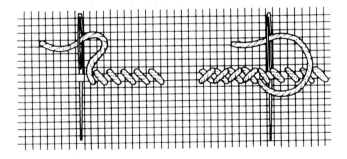

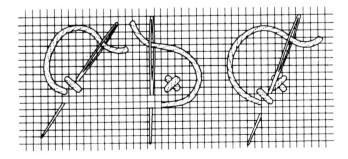

● When stitching large areas of one colour, such as a background, it is easiest to work in horizontal rows. Working from right to left, complete the first row of evenly spaced diagonal stitches over the number of threads specified in the project instructions. Then, working from left to right, repeat the process. Continue in this way to fill the area, following the chart, making sure each stitch crosses in the same direction.

● When stitching diagonal lines in a design, work downwards, completing each stitch before moving to the next. Make sure all the crosses look the same, with the top of the cross going in the same direction. When starting a project always begin to embroider at the centre of the design and work outwards to ensure that the design will be placed centrally on the fabric.

THREE-QUARTER CROSS STITCH

Some fractional stitches are used on certain projects in this book; although they strike fear into the hearts of less experienced stitchers they are not difficult to master, and give a more natural line in certain instances. Should you find it difficult to pierce the centre of the Aida block, simply use a sharp needle to make a small hole in the centre first, before making the stitch.

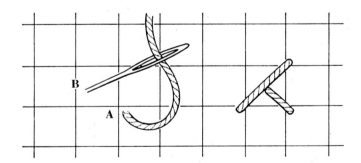

● To work a three-quarter cross, bring the needle up at point A and down through the centre of the square at B. Later, the diagonal back stitch finishes the stitch. A chart square with two different symbols separated by a diagonal line requires two 'three-quarter' stitches. Backstitch will later finish the square.

A clear distinction needs to be made between three-quarter cross stitches and half cross stitches. A three-quarter stitch occupies half of a square diagonally. A half cross stitch is like a normal cross stitch, but only the top diagonal stitch is worked, to give a more delicate effect to the finished design. Stitches worked in this way are indicated quite clearly on the colour keys next to each chart with their own symbols.

BACKSTITCH

Backstitch is used in the projects to give emphasis to a particular foldline, an outline or a shadow. The stitches are worked over the same number of threads as the cross stitch, forming continuous straight or diagonal lines.

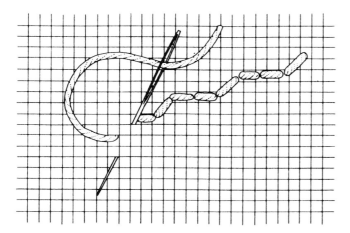

● Make the first stitch from left to right; pass the needle behind the fabric and bring it out one stitch length ahead to the left. Repeat and continue in this way along the line.

FRENCH KNOTS

This stitch is shown on some of the diagrams by a small dot. Where there are several french knots featured in the design, the dots have been omitted from the diagrams to avoid confusion. Where this occurs you should refer to the instructions of the project and the colour photograph.

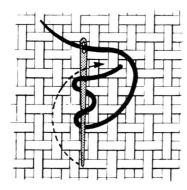

● To work a french knot, bring your needle and cotton out slightly to the right of where you want your knot to be. Wind the thread once or twice around the needle, depending on how big you want your knot to be, and insert the needle to the left of the point where you brought it out.

Be careful not to pull too hard or the knot will disappear through the fabric. The instructions state the number of strands of cotton to be used for the french knots.

FINISHING

MITRING A CORNER

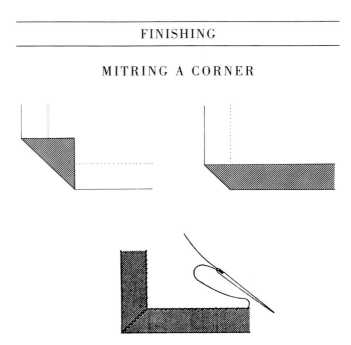

● Press a single hem to the wrong side, the same as the measurement given in the instructions. Open the hem out again and fold the corner of the fabric inwards as shown on the diagram. Refold the hem to the wrong side along the pressed line, and slip stitch in place.

BINDING AN EDGE

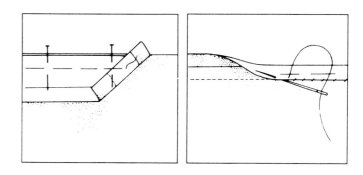

1 Open out the turning on one edge of the bias binding and pin in position on the right side of the fabric, matching the fold to the seamline. Fold over the cut end of the binding. Finish the binding by overlapping the starting point by about 12mm (½in). Baste and then machine stitch along the seamline to secure.

2 Fold the binding over the raw edge to the wrong side. Then baste to secure and, using matching sewing thread, neatly hem the binding in place to finish. Finally, press the binding for a neat edge.

PIPED SEAMS

Contrasting piping adds a special decorative finish to a seam, brightening up a plain-coloured fabric, and looks particularly attractive on items such as cushions and cosies. You can also use it to highlight a colour in your embroidery.

You can cover piping cord with either bias-cut fabric of your choice or a bias binding; alternatively, ready-covered piping cord is available in several widths and many colours.

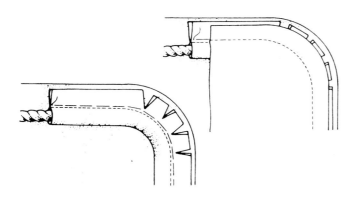

1 To apply piping to your fabric, pin and baste it to the right side of the fabric, with seam lines matching. Clip into the seam allowance where necessary and trim excess fabric.

2 With right sides together, place the second piece of fabric on top, enclosing the piping inside. Baste and then either hand stitch the piping in place or machine stitch, using a zipper foot. Stitch as close to the piping as possible, covering the first line of stitching.

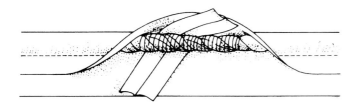

3 To join ends of piping cord together, first overlap the two ends by about 2.5cm (1in). Unpick the two cut ends of bias to reveal the cord. Join the bias strip as shown. Trim and press the seam open. Unravel and splice the two ends of the cord. Fold the bias strip over it, and finish basting around the edge.

MOUNTING EMBROIDERY

The cardboard should be cut to the size of the finished embroidery, with an extra 6mm (¼in) added all round to allow for the recess in the frame.

LIGHTWEIGHT FABRICS

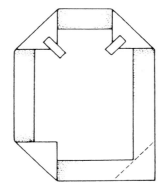
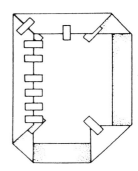

1 Place embroidery face down, with the cardboard centred on top, and basting and pencil lines matching. Begin by folding over the fabric at each corner and securing it with masking tape.

2 Working first on one side and then the other, fold over the fabric on all sides and secure it firmly with pieces of masking tape, placed about 2.5cm (1in) apart. Also neaten the mitred corners with masking tape, pulling the fabric tightly to give a firm, smooth finish.

HEAVIER FABRICS

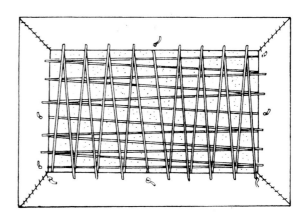

● Lay the embroidery face down, with the cardboard centred on top; fold over the edges of the fabric on opposite sides, making mitred folds at the corners, and lace across, using strong thread. Repeat on the other two sides. Finally, pull up the fabric firmly over the cardboard. Overstitch the mitred corners.

BLESS
THIS
HOUSE

Whether you prefer a thatched cottage, with
roses around the door and a garden
overflowing with pretty flowers, or a small
stone house with smoke curling from the
chimney, houses and cottages make an
excellent stitching theme. This chapter
includes traditional homely samplers together
with trinket boxes and pictures.

HOUSE AND GARDEN SAMPLER

YOU WILL NEED

For a Sampler measuring 23cm (9in) square
(unframed):

*35cm (14in) square of white linen, 26 threads to
2.5cm (1in)*
*Stranded embroidery cotton in the colours given in
the panel*
*23cm (9in) square of 3mm (1/8in) cardboard for
mounting the embroidery*
*23cm (9in) square of lightweight synthetic
wadding (batting)*
Strong thread for securing the mounted fabric
Picture frame of your choice
No26 tapestry needle

•

Following the alphabet given with the sampler,
select your chosen initials and, using a soft pencil,
draw them on the chart. For three initials, ignore the
centre diamond and experiment with the spacing,
positioning them within the central area. You may
prefer to add the date of the embroidery, or a longer
dedication. In which case, ignore the two hearts and
the two outer diamonds and use the whole of the
lower area. You will find it easier to follow if this is
charted on a separate piece of graph paper, matching
the grid to that given in the book. If you do remove
the hearts, it would be nice to work the embroidery
in red, or perhaps the blue, from the border. Whichever colour you use, it will be helpful to chart your
wording as a guide before working the embroidery.

THE EMBROIDERY

With the prepared fabric stretched in a frame, see
page 9, and the centre lines basted both ways,
begin the embroidery. Using two strands of thread
in the needle and carefully following the chart,
complete the embroidery, working one cross stitch
over two threads of fabric. Remember that with very
openweave fabrics it is important not to strand the
thread from one area to another, otherwise it will
show through on the right side. Begin and finish
threads underneath an embroidered area, and trim
all loose ends when finishing.

Remove the finished embroidery from the frame,
but do not take out the basting threads at this stage.
Steam press on the wrong side.

FRAMING THE SAMPLER

A thin layer of batting is placed between the cardboard and the embroidery. In this case it helps to
give an opaque quality to the openweave linen. To
centre the cardboard over the embroidery, first
mark the centre line of the cardboard both ways,
using a soft pencil. Similarly, mark the batting by
placing a pin at the central point on each side.

Lay the embroidery face down; centre the batting
on top, and then the cardboard, with basting, pins
and pencil lines matching.

Working on one side and then the opposite side,
fold over the edges of the fabric on all sides and
secure with masking tape, see page 13, first
removing the pins. Neaten the corners by folding
them in to form a mitre and secure with masking
tape. Remove the basting threads.

Insert the glass and mounted embroidery into
your picture frame; add the backing board provided, and secure with picture tacks. Cover the
tacks with broad sticky tape to neaten.

HOUSE AND GARDEN ▶			
	DMC	ANCHOR	MADEIRA
⊟ Ecru	Ecru	387	Ecru
◩ Pale yellow	744	301	0112
◪ Naples yellow	677	886	2207
↑ Soft yellow	743	301	0113
◆ Deep gold	972	303	0107
▯ Pale salmon pink	352	9	0303
✦ Salmon pink	351	10	0214
⊡ Brick red	350	11	0213
⒮ Pale blue	927	849	1708
⊙ Blue	597	168	1110
◻ Pale green	523	215	1208
⊡ Olive green	732	281	1612
⤓ Khaki	3012	854	1606

Note: bks window sashes in pale salmon pink.

Home Sweet Home

The traditional text of this *Home Sweet Home* sampler, embellished with a striking border, will help to make your house a home.

The sampler uses a spectrum of sumptuous jewel shades – jade and emerald greens, pinks and purples – to complement the composition and create a vivid embroidery. The pattern of the deep border is richly resplendent, making the perfect frame for the traditional-style lettering.

HOME SWEET HOME

YOU WILL NEED

For the Home Sweet Home sampler, with a design area measuring 23cm (9in) square, or 125 stitches each way, here in a frame measuring 36cm (14½in) square:

*33cm (13in) square of white, 14-count
Aida fabric
Stranded embroidery cotton in the colours given
in the panel
No24 tapestry needle
Strong thread, for lacing across the back
Cardboard, for mounting, sufficient to fit into the
frame recess
Frame of your choice*

•

THE EMBROIDERY

Prepare the fabric and stretch it in a frame as explained on page 9. Following the chart, start the embroidery at the centre of the design, using two strands of embroidery cotton in the needle. Work each stitch over one block of fabric in each direction, making sure that all the top crosses run in the same direction and each row is worked into the same holes as the top or bottom of the row before, so that you do not leave a space between the rows. For a simple sampler, the words 'Home Sweet Home' could be worked with just the inner border around the outside and for the finishing touch, you might add a row of stitching in dark magenta one square away from the inner border.

MAKING UP

Gently steam press the work on the wrong side and mount it as explained on page 13. Choose your own mount and frame from the large selection available in the shops or use one of the many framing services available to put the finishing touch to your work.

HOME SWEET HOME ▶	DMC	ANCHOR	MADEIRA
: Light pink	776	73	0606
% Dark pink	899	40	0609
> Light mauve	3608	86	0709
+ Dark mauve	718	88	0707
v Yellow	743	301	0113
x Light green	320	215	1310
− Medium green	367	216	1312
s Dark green	319	217	1313

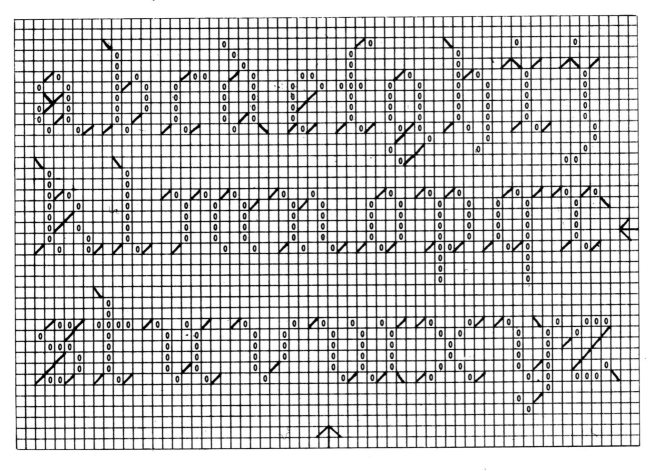

Alternative alphabet

Little Houses

Small motifs of cottages make delightful pictures, trinkets, gifts and cards – suitable for many occasions. They also make an ideal starting point for the newcomer to cross stitch as they are quick and easy to stitch. Five separate designs are given here, each made up in a different format.

LITTLE HOUSES

YOU WILL NEED

For each design you will require the following:

13cm (5¼in) square of linen (see individual item for the thread count)
Stranded embroidery cotton in the colours given in the appropriate panel
No26 tapestry needle

For the Gift Tag, measuring 5cm (2in) square:

Antique white, 18-count Aida fabric
Gift tag (for suppliers, see page 220)

For the Key Ring, measuring 4cm (1½in) in diameter:

Antique white, 18-count Aida fabric
Key ring (for suppliers, see page 220)

For the Oval Box, with a lid measuring approximately 7cm × 5cm (2¾in × 2in):

Antique white, 18-count Aida fabric
Soft pink porcelain box (for suppliers see page 220)

For the Round Box, measuring approximately 6.5cm (2½in) in diameter:

Antique white, 14-count Aida fabric
Round ivory porcelain box (for suppliers, see page 220)

For the Card, measuring 10cm × 6.5cm (4in × 2½in), with an oval opening:

Antique white, 14-count Aida fabric
Purchased card (for suppliers, see page 220)

•

THE EMBROIDERY

Each design uses only a small amount of fabric, which makes these projects an ideal way of using up off-cuts. On the other hand, if you have no odd pieces of fabric, you may prefer to embroider designs in batches – gift tag, key ring and oval box, or round box and card – to avoid waste.

For each design, prepare the fabric as described on page 9, and mark the horizontal and vertical centre lines with basting stitches in a light-coloured thread. Set the fabric in a hoop and count out from the centre to start stitching at a point convenient to you. Work all cross stitches first, making sure that all top stitches run in the same direction. Finally, work all backstitch details.

For the gift tag, key ring and oval porcelain box, use one strand of embroidery cotton in the needle when making cross stitches and also for backstitching. For the round porcelain box and card, use two strands of thread in the needle when making the cross stitches, and one for backstitching.

Gently handwash the finished piece, if necessary, and lightly press with a steam iron on the wrong side. Follow the manufacturer's instructions for assembly.

OVAL BOX ▼

Cross	Half Cross		DMC	ANCHOR	MADEIRA
▼		Apple green	368	261	1310
⊘		Soft blue	3752	343	1001
□		Light salmon pink	761	8	0404
•		White	White	2	White
Z		Light golden brown	612	832	2108
◥		Medium steel grey	646	815	1811
X		Medium straw	3046	373	2103
⊏		Light straw	3047	886	2205
◪		Medium grey green	522	860	1602
+		Medium pink brown	3064	378	2310
<		Ecru	Ecru	926	2101
	◹	Tan	437	368	2011
0		Very light grey green	524	858	1511
		Medium golden brown*	611	898	2107

Note: bks around window frames and panes with white, and around window frames, door and fence with medium golden brown (used for bks only).*

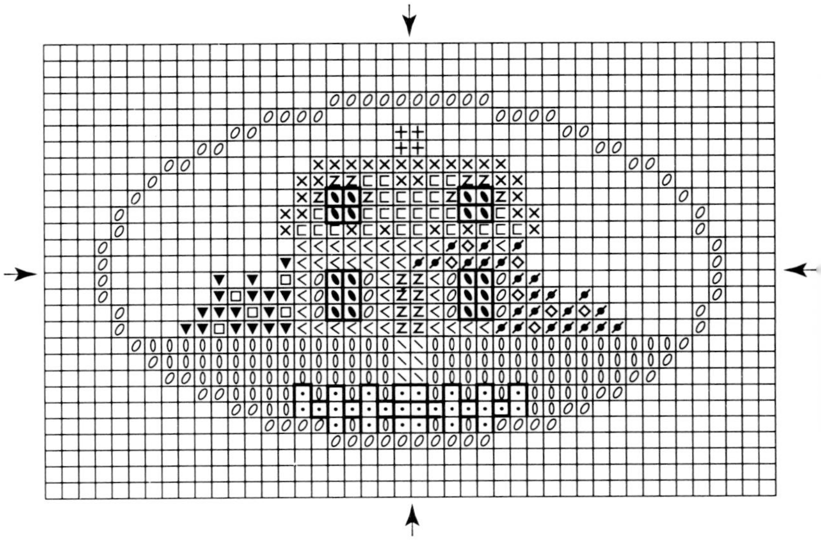

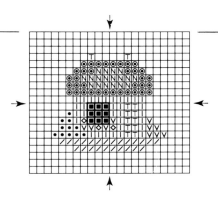

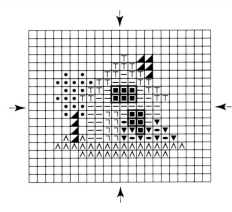

GIFT TAG ▲			DMC	ANCHOR	MADEIRA
Cross	Half Cross				
◉		Medium grey beige	3022	8581	1903
N		Light grey beige	3023	392	1902
T		Medium golden tan	420	889	2010
■		Dark steel grey	645	400	1811
●		Clear green	3363	262	1311
◇		Medium salmon pink	760	9	0405
V		Light grey green	523	859	1512
I		Beige	3033	392	1903
	╱	Very light gold brown	613	831	2109
		White*	White	2	White

Note: bks window panes with one strand of white (used for bks only).*

KEY RING ▲			DMC	ANCHOR	MADEIRA
Cross	Half Cross				
T		Medium golden tan	420	889	2010
■		Dark steel grey	645	400	1811
●		Clear green	3363	262	1311
▲		Medium golden brown	611	898	2107
˥		Red brown	433	371	2303
▼		Apple green	368	261	1310
◖		Medium antique blue	932	920	1710
▭		Soft pink brown	3773	882	2312
	⋀	Light grey green	523	859	1512
		White*	White	2	White

Note: bks window frames and panes with one strand of white (used for bks only).*

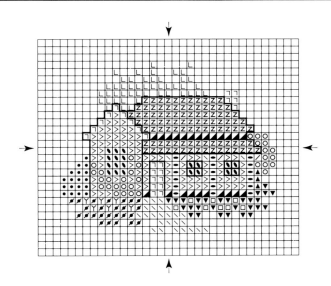

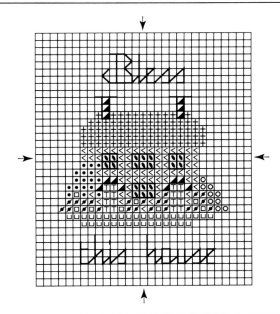

ROUND BOX ▲			DMC	ANCHOR	MADEIRA
Cross	Half Cross				
●		Clear green	3363	262	1311
◢		Medium golden brown	611	898	2107
˥		Red brown	433	371	2303
▼		Apple green	368	261	1310
◖		Medium antique blue	932	920	1710
▢		Light salmon pink	761	8	0404
Z		Light golden brown	612	832	2108
◥		Medium steel grey	646	815	1811
◤		Medium grey green	522	860	1602
	◫	Tan	437	368	2011
	L	Very light grey green	524	858	1511
O		Light olive green	3053	216	1513
Y		Yellow	744	301	0112
▷		Light silver grey	762	397	1804
▲		Dark golden brown	610	905	1914
		White*	White	2	White

Note: bks with white (used for bks only) around window frames and panes, and dark golden brown for walls and roof.*

CARD ▲			DMC	ANCHOR	MADEIRA
Cross	Half Cross				
T		Medium golden tan	420	889	2010
●		Clear green	3363	262	1311
◢		Medium golden brown	611	898	2107
	⊔	Apple green	368	261	1310
▢		Light salmon pink	761	8	0404
◥		Medium steel grey	646	815	1811
O		Light olive green	3053	216	1513
		White*	White	2	White
		Dark steel grey*	645	400	1811
		Dark golden brown*	610	905	1914

Note: bks with white for window panes, dark steel grey* for lettering, and dark golden brown* (all used for bks only) for window frames and chimneys.*

Traditional Cottage Sampler

The traditional sampler with its
border, floral motifs and alphabet has
enjoyed a tremendous revival in
popularity in recent years.
This sampler is a fresh approach to
the theme featuring delicate colours,
a heartwarming quotation and a
vignette of a thatched cottage set
in a pretty garden.

TRADITIONAL COTTAGE SAMPLER

YOU WILL NEED

For the Traditional Cottage sampler, set in a frame measuring 20cm × 25cm (8in × 10in):

25cm × 30cm (10in × 12in) of antique white, 18-count Aida fabric
Stranded embroidery cotton in the colours given in the panel
No 26 tapestry needle
Wooden frame, as specified above
Strong thread and cardboard, for mounting

•

THE EMBROIDERY

Prepare the fabric as described on page 9; find the centre by folding, and mark the horizontal and vertical centre lines with basting stitches in a light-coloured thread. Set the fabric in a frame, and count out from the centre to start stitching at a point convenient to you.

One thread of cotton was used in the needle for cross stitches and one for backstitch throughout this design. Work all cross stitiches first, and then the half crosses, taking them over one block of fabric. Make sure that all top stitches run in the same direction. (Please note that some three-quarter stitches are used in this design – an explanation of how to do these stitches is given on page 11.) Finally, work all backstitch details.

FINISHING

Gently handwash the finished piece, if necessary, and lightly press with a steam iron on the wrong side. Stretch and mount the embroidery as explained on page 13. Insert it into the frame. A fairly traditional style of wooden frame looks most suitable with this type of design.

TRADITIONAL COTTAGE ▶			DMC	ANCHOR	MADEIRA
Cross	Half Cross				
◨		Silver grey	415	398	1803
		Dark grey blue*	926	779	1707
☒		Light grey blue	927	849	1708
Ⲥ		Very light grey blue	928	900	1709
Ⓩ		Light shell pink	3713	48	0502
Ⓝ		Light salmon pink	761	8	0404
▲		Medium salmon pink	760	9	0405
●		Clear green	3363	262	1311
Ⓞ		Medium grey green	522	859	1513
Ⓛ	·	Light grey green	524	858	1511
◎		Soft antique violet	3042	869	0807
⊟	◥	Apple green	368	261	1310
◪		Medium golden brown	611	898	2107
Ⴠ		Light tan	437	362	2012
⊞		Dark brown	839	360	1914
◇		Olive green	3053	844	1510
Ⅰ		Very light beige	3033	387	2001
Ⅴ		Beige	3782	388	1906
∕		Light steel grey	648	900	1814
Ⲩ		Medium steel grey	647	8581	1813
▪		Very dark steel grey	645	400	1811

Note: bks inner and outer border and lettering in dark grey blue* (used for bks only), hearts in medium salmon pink, flourishes with hearts in medium grey green, window panes in white* (used for bks only) and roof, chimneys and door in medium golden brown.

View of a Cottage

A pretty thatched cottage, a sleepy cat, and a colourful butterfly flitting among the summer flowers are all combined in this idyllic and nostalgic village scene, framed to hang on your wall.

VIEW OF A COTTAGE

YOU WILL NEED

For the View of a Cottage Picture, measuring
38cm × 32cm (15¼in × 12¾in):

48cm × 42cm (19¼in × 16¾in) ivory,
11-count Aida fabric
Stranded embroidery cotton in the colours given in
the panel
No24 tapestry needle
Strong thread, for lacing across the back
Frame of your choice

•

THE EMBROIDERY

Prepare the fabric and stretch it in a frame, as
explained on page 9. Following the chart, start the
embroidery at the centre of the design, using three
strands of embroidery cotton in the needle. Work
each stitch over one block of fabric in each direction. Make sure that the top crosses run in the same
direction.

Using backstitch, work the outlines and markings
using one strand of cotton in the appropriate colour.

ASSEMBLING THE PICTURE

Gently steam press the work and mount it as
explained on page 13. Lace the embroidery over the
mount, following the instructions on page 13. Choose
a frame in a colour to complement the embroidery
colours, and assemble the frame according to the
manufacturer's instructions.

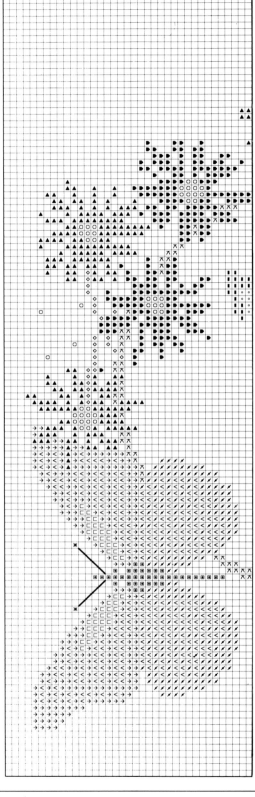

TOP

VIEW OF A COTTAGE		DMC	ANCHOR	MADEIRA			DMC	ANCHOR	MADEIRA
⊡	Light green	704	254	1308	▶ Light grey-mauve	3042	870	0807
⊙	Green	702	238	1306	◁ Pale blue	341	117	901
⊡	Moss green	470	266	1502	▼ Mauve	340	109	0902
▼	Dark green	986	244	1404	△ Beige	642	392	1906
⊡	Grey-green	522	859	1513	○ Grey	648	900	1814
⊡	Lemon yellow	307	289	0104	▣ Dark grey	317	400	1714
◣	Golden yellow	743	891	0113	→ Khaki	833	945	2203
✳	Golden brown	782	374	2212	↖ Dark sand	831	888	2201

BOTTOM

		DMC	ANCHOR	MADEIRA
⊡	Dark brown	801	358	2007
⊠	Red	606	335	0209
↓	Tangerine	741	314	0201
♡	Pink	604	26	0614
⊠	Fuchsia	718	88	0707
⊓	Apricot	738	311	2301
⊠	Flesh pink	754	6	0305
△	Very pale salmon	3779	881	2313

		DMC	ANCHOR	MADEIRA
⊟	Cream	739	885	2014
◣	Dark orange	922	324	0310
⠶	White	White	1	White
▲	Black	310	403	Black

Note: bks outline the cottage windows, the cat's whiskers, features and paws, and the butterfly's antennae in black.

GLORIOUS GARDENS

Cheer yourself up in the cold winter months by stitching a delightful garden scene. Choose from a rose garden, a cottage garden, or even a vegetable garden, all of which capture the colours of sunny spring and summer flowers.

SPRING COTTAGE

YOU WILL NEED

For the Spring Cottage Picture, set in a mount with
a cut-out measuring 16.5cm × 21.5cm
(6½in × 8½in):

*30cm × 35cm (12in × 14in) of antique white,
14-count Aida fabric
Stranded embroidery cotton in the colours given in
the panel
No 26 tapestry needle
Wooden frame, measuring 26cm × 30cm
(10⅜in × 12in)
Rectangular mount, cut to fit the frame, with
cut-out as specified above
Strong thread and cardboard, for mounting*

•

THE EMBROIDERY

Prepare the fabric as described on page 9; find the
centre by folding, and mark the horizontal and
vertical centre lines with basting stitches in a light-
coloured thread. Set the fabric in a frame or hoop
and count out from the centre to start stitching at a
point convenient to you.

Two threads of cotton were used in the needle
for cross stitches and one for backstitch, *unless*
otherwise stated on the colour key. Work all full
cross stitches first, and then the half crosses, taking
them over one block of fabric. Make sure that all
top stitches run in the same direction. Finally, work
all backstitch details.

FINISHING

Gently handwash the finished piece, if necessary,
and lightly press with a steam iron on the wrong
side. Finally, stretch and mount the embroidery
as explained on page 13. Insert it into the frame,
behind the rectangular mount. A subtle, wooden
frame has been used for this seasonal cottage
picture, and the colour of the mount has been
especially selected to echo colours predominant in
the design.

SPRING COTTAGE ▶			DMC	ANCHOR	MADEIRA
Cross	**Half Cross**				
⊞		White	White	2	White
⊙		Medium olive green	3053	859	1510
▲		Dark beige grey	640	903	1905
▽		Medium beige grey	642	392	1906
⌷		Light beige grey	644	830	1907
◉		Dark olive green	3052	844	1509
◪		Dark brown	839	360	1914
⊘		Medium salmon pink	760	9	0405
⋀		Light salmon pink	761	8	0404
◼		Dark grey	844	401	1810
Ⴀ		Golden tan	420	375	2104
◗		Light blue grey	927	849	1708
◪	⧸	Medium grey green	522	859	1513
⋅	⧄	Very light grey green	524	858	1511
⌊		Light yellow	744	301	0112
⊻		Very light yellow	745	300	0111
	⧅	Light tan	437	362	2012
	⊏	Very light tan	738	942	2013
◇		Apple green	368	261	1310
⊙		Clear green	3363	262	1311
⊔		Light clear green	3364	843	1603
⊟		Beige	3033	387	2001
	⋈	Very soft blue	3753	158	1014
⊠		Golden brown	612	832	2108
		Dark golden brown*	611	898	2107

*Note: bks roof, house, door and birds with one strand only of dark golden
brown* (used for bks only) in the needle, and window panes with two strands
of white; when using very soft blue, stitch with one strand only; very light
green is used for cross stitches in the background and half cross stitches in
the foreground; very light tan, apple green, and very soft blue are used for
half cross stitches only.*

Cottage Garden Pictures

This tiny trio features a little cottage and garden, a closer view of a pretty front door framed by a climbing rose, and a wheatsheaf. Together or individually, they would add a touch of elegance to a dressing table.

COTTAGE GARDEN PICTURES

YOU WILL NEED

For the Wheatsheaf Picture, measuring approximately 4.5cm × 3.5cm (1³/₄in × 1³/₈in):

6.5cm × 5cm (2¹/₂in × 2in) of white, 22-count Aida fabric
Stranded embroidery cotton in the colours given in the panel
No26 tapestry needle
Strong thread, for lacing across the back
Oval silver-plated frame (for suppliers, see page 220)

For the Cottage Garden Picture, measuring approximately 7.5cm × 6cm (3in × 2³/₈in):

9.5cm × 8cm (3³/₄in × 3¹/₄in) of white, 22-count Aida fabric
Stranded embroidery cotton in the colours given in the panel
No26 tapestry needle
Strong thread, for lacing across the back
Oval silver-plated frame (for suppliers, see page 220)

For the Rose-framed Door Picture, measuring approximately 10cm × 8cm (4in × 3¹/₄in):

12cm × 10cm (4³/₄in × 4in) of white, 22-count Aida fabric
Stranded embroidery cotton in the colours given in the panel
No26 tapestry needle
Strong thread, for lacing across the back
Oval silver-plated frame (for suppliers, see page 220)

•

THE EMBROIDERY

If you are stitching all the motifs, or several copies of one motif, you can economize by using just one piece of fabric, measuring approximately 25cm × 15cm (10in × 6in). Make sure that you leave an adequate amount of space for your purposes around each design. Stretch the fabric in a hoop or frame, as explained on page 9. Following the appropriate chart, start each embroidery at the centre of the design, using one strand of embroidery cotton in the needle. Work each stitch over one block of fabric in each direction. Make sure that the top crosses run in the same direction. Once all the motifs have been embroidered, gently steam press on the wrong side, and cut out each one leaving a generous margin of fabric for framing.

FRAMING THE PICTURES

Mount each picture by stretching it over the oval of card provided, lacing across the back with strong thread (see page 13). Frame each one following the manufacturer's instructions.

COTTAGE GARDEN ▼		DMC	ANCHOR	MADEIRA
⊞	Beige	738	372	2013
◨	Green	703	238	1307
⊠	Dark green	700	227	1305
✳	Bright red	606	333	208
↓	Pink	604	55	614
▽	Lavender	340	109	90
◭	Fuchsia pink	3607	87	0706
◩	Pale blue	3325	159	1002
◿	Yellow	444	290	104
⊙	Tangerine	741	314	0201
◱	Brick red	356	5975	401
■	Black	310	403	Black
↑	Pale grey	762	234	1804
⊡	White	White	1	White

Note: bks the door and window frames in black.

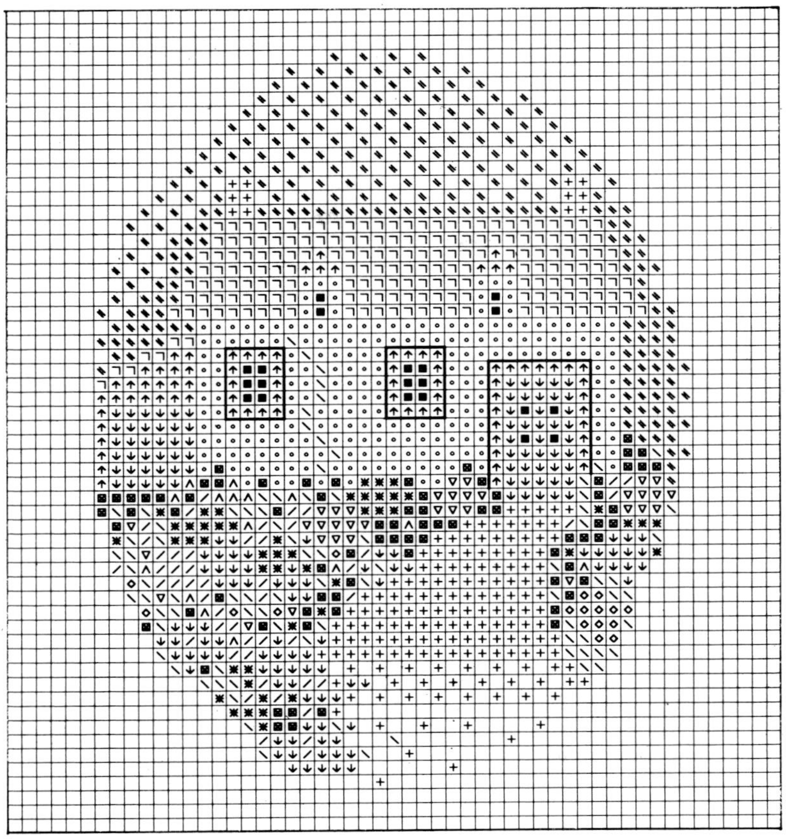

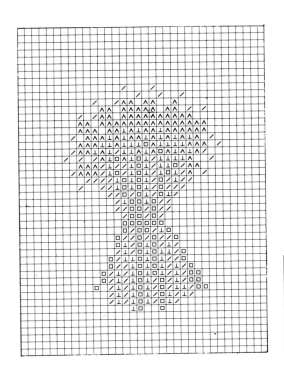

ROSE-FRAMED DOOR ▲	DMC	ANCHOR	MADEIRA
⌐ Light green	913	204	1212
◨ Green	793	238	1307
⊡ Dark green	701	227	1305
◢ Light grey	928	234	1709
◰ Dark grey	413	400	1714
↓ Cornflower blue	793	121	906
▼ Bright red	606	333	209
◦ Pink	604	55	614
△ Fuchsia pink	3607	87	708
◺ Lavender	209	109	803
◣ Gold	729	890	2209
— Beige	738	372	2013
⸬ Light brown	3064	883	2312
⊞ Brown	801	358	2007
◇ Orange	740	314	202
▪ Light yellow	445	288	103
∧ Yellow	307	290	104
■ Black	310	403	Black

WHEATSHEAF ◄	DMC	ANCHOR	MADEIRA
⊡ Tan	434	310	2009
◿ Light tan	680	890	2209
⊥ Beige	738	372	2013
∧ Gold	437	891	2012

A Touch of Summer

The summer garden is a riot of colour and fragrance, attracting natural visitors, such as brightly-coloured butterflies; the summer flowers and fruit at the front of this design lead the eye to the view of a cottage garden behind, complete with a rose-covered arch.

A TOUCH OF SUMMER

YOU WILL NEED

For the Summer picture, set in a mount with a cut-out measuring 12.5cm × 16cm (5in × 6¼in):

32.5cm × 36cm (13in × 14¼in) of antique white, 18-count Aida fabric
Stranded embroidery cotton in the colours given in the panel
No26 tapestry needle
Wooden frame measuring 22.5cm × 26cm (8¾in × 10¼in)
Rectangular mount, cut to fit the frame, with cut-out as specified above
Strong thread and cardboard, for mounting

•

THE EMBROIDERY

Prepare the fabric as described on page 9; find the centre by folding, and mark the horizontal and vertical centre lines with basting stitches in a light-coloured thread. Set the fabric in a frame or hoop

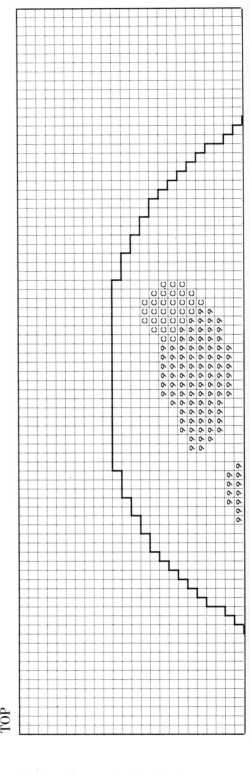

TOP

A TOUCH OF SUMMER ▶				DMC	ANCHOR	MADEIRA
Cross	**Half Cross**					
•			White	White	2	White
−			Very light pink	819	271	0501
O			Pale shell pink	3713	48	0502
P			Light salmon pink	761	8	0404
▲			Medium salmon pink	760	9	0405
Y			Medium yellow	744	301	0112
C			Light yellow	745	300	0111
B	⟋		Light golden brown	613	831	2109
			Dark golden brown*	611	898	2107
●			Clear green	3363	262	1602
L			Medium grey green	522	860	1513
V	⟍		Very light grey green	524	858	1511
S			Light khaki	372	853	2110
■			Medium olive green	3052	859	1509
R			Light olive green	3053	844	1510
6			Light cornflower blue	794	175	0907
△			Medium cornflower blue	793	176	0906
X			Apple green	368	240	1310
8			Medium khaki	370	855	2112
U			Light grass green	471	253	1414
=			Dark pink	3712	1023	0406
⌁			Light orange	402	1047	2307
▼			Dark golden brown	611	898	2107
	9		Very pale blue	3753	1031	1001
			Dark grey*	646	815	1809

Note: bks the border outline in clear green, fence in dark grey, and strawberry flowers, daisies and butterfly in dark golden brown* (starred outline colours are not indicated by symbols on the chart). Using dark golden brown, make either tiny stitches or french knots to form the dots in the wings and feelers of the butterfly.*

(see page 9) and count out from the centre to start stitching at a point convenient to you.

One thread of cotton was used in the needle for cross stitches and for backstitch. Work all full cross stitches first, and then the half crosses. The half cross stitches have their own individual symbols on the chart; for each half cross, work only the top stitch of the two that make up a full cross stitch, to produce a more delicate effect.

Take both half and full crosses over one block of

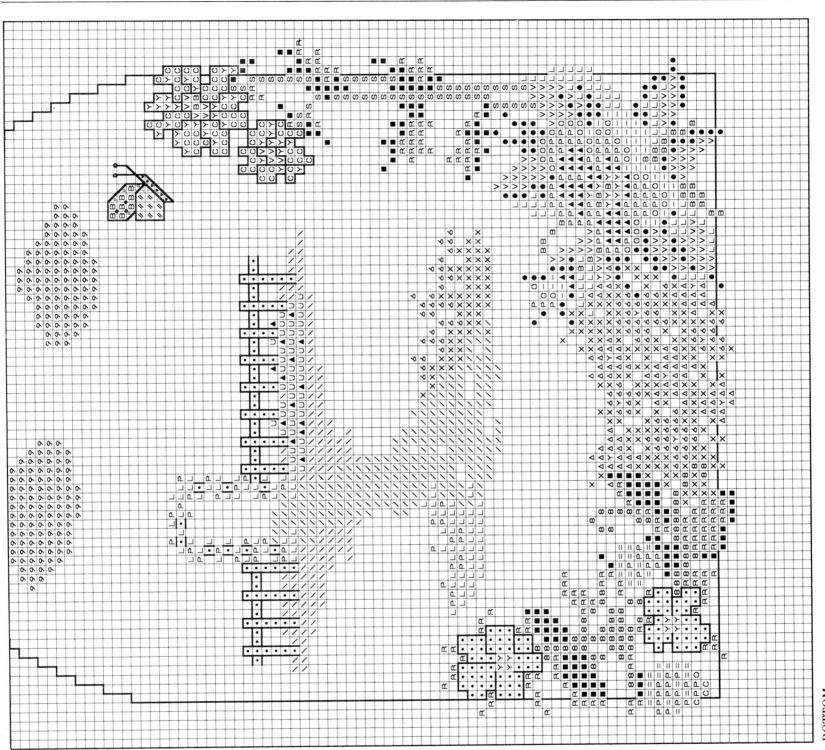

the fabric, making sure that all top stitches run in the same direction (if top stitches run in different directions, they will reflect the light in opposite directions and the work will look uneven). Finally, work all backstitch details.

FINISHING

Gently handwash the finished piece, if necessary, and lightly press with a steam iron on the wrong side. Stretch and mount the embroidery as explained on page 13. Insert it into the frame, behind the rectangular mount.

For this seasonal picture, the colour of the mount has been specially selected to echo colours and tones predominant in the design.

Rose Cottage

Walk down the pathway of this
English cottage garden and take a
step back in time. In your
imagination, smell the sweet scent of
lavender and absorb the colours and
peacefulness of a bygone era.
The rambling roses around the cottage
door are embroidered with clusters of
french knots to give extra depth and
texture to this nostalgic design. It has
been set in a deep frame, but an
alternative idea would be to surround
it with a double mount, to add to the
sense of perspective.

ROSE COTTAGE

YOU WILL NEED

For the Rose Cottage, with a design area measuring 19.5cm × 15cm (7¾in × 6in), or 119 stitches by 85 stitches, here in a frame measuring 23cm × 18.5cm (9in × 7½in):

*30cm × 25cm (12in × 10in) of white,
14-count Aida fabric
Stranded embroidery cotton in the colours given
in the panel
No24 tapestry needle
Strong thread, for lacing across the back
Cardboard for mounting, sufficient to fit in the
frame recess
Frame and mount of your choice*

•

THE EMBROIDERY

Prepare the piece of fabric and stretch it in a frame as explained on page 9. Following the chart, start the embroidery at the centre of the design, using two strands of embroidery cotton in the needle. Work each stitch over a block of fabric in each direction. Make sure that all the top crosses run in the same direction and each row is worked into the same holes as the top or bottom of the row before, so that you do not leave a space between the rows.

Using backstitch, work all the outlines and markings with one strand of dark green cotton. Work the roses in clusters of medium and dark coloured pink french knots, using six strands of cotton in the needle and winding the cotton around the needle either once or twice, varying this so that some clusters of roses stand out more than others, to create a three-dimensional effect.

MAKING UP

Steam press the work on the wrong side and mount it as explained on page 13. Choose a mount and frame that are in keeping with the 'Olde Worlde' charm of the picture.

ROSE COTTAGE		DMC	ANCHOR	MADEIRA			DMC	ANCHOR	MADEIRA
╱	Light pink	776	73	0606	c	Cream	746	275	0101
:	Medium pink	894	26	0408	+	Light gold	676	887	2208
<	Dark pink	891	29	0412	n	Medium gold	729	890	2209
\	Light mauve	210	108	0803	g	Dark gold	680	901	2210
>	Medium mauve	208	111	0804	v	Yellow	743	301	0113
%	Dark mauve	550	101	0714	‡	Light blue	799	130	0910

		DMC	ANCHOR	MADEIRA			DMC	ANCHOR	MADEIRA
=	Dark blue	798	131	0911	?	Dark brown	829	906	2106
−	Light green	3348	264	1409	o	Light grey	762	234	1804
⌐	Medium green	3347	266	1408	z	Dark grey	414	399	1801
s	Dark green	3345	268	1406					
@	Darkest green	936	263	1507					
x	Light brown	434	365	2009					

'In a Cottage Garden' Pillow

This design is reminiscent of
traditional sampler styles, with its
rows of stylized flowers and leaves,
but it has been interpreted in the style
of the typical English cottage garden
and made up as a small pillow.
To carry the garden theme still further
you could insert a small amount of
scented potpourri into the pillow.

'IN A COTTAGE GARDEN'

YOU WILL NEED

For the Pillow, measuring 23cm (9in) square,
excluding the lace trim:

30cm (12in) square of white, 18-count Aida fabric
Stranded embroidery cotton in the colours given in
the panel
No 26 tapestry needle
1.1m (1¹⁄₃yds) of gathered broderie anglaise,
3cm (1¹⁄₄in) wide
25cm (10in) square of backing fabric
4 white ribbon roses
Polyester filling
Pot pourri (optional)

•

THE EMBROIDERY

Prepare the fabric as described on page 9; find the
centre by folding, and mark the horizontal and
vertical centre lines with basting stitches in a light-
coloured thread. Set the fabric in a frame or hoop
(see page 9), and count out from the centre to
start stitching at a point convenient to you.

One thread of cotton was used in the needle for
cross stitches and for backstitch throughout the
design. Work all cross stitches first, making sure
that all top stitches run in the same direction.
Finally, work all backstitch details.

MAKING THE PILLOW

Gently handwash the finished piece, if necessary,
and lightly press with a steam iron on the wrong
side. Trim the embroidered fabric to measure 25cm
(10in) square. Pin the broderie anglaise to the right
side of the embroidery, with the decorative edge
facing inwards. Trim the ends, if necessary, and
join them with a neat french seam.

Gathering it slightly at the corners, baste the
broderie anglaise in place, lying just inside the
12mm (½in) seam allowance. With right sides
together, pin and stitch the backing fabric and
embroidered piece together, leaving a gap of 5cm
(2in) at one side.

Clip the corners; turn the cover right side out,
and fill with polyester, adding the pot pourri if this
is to be included. Slipstitch the opening, and finish
by stitching a ribbon rose in each corner of the
cushion.

IN A COTTAGE GARDEN ▶		DMC	ANCHOR	MADEIRA
⬙	Medium grey green	522	860	1513
◎	Light grey green	523	859	1512
·	Very light grey green	524	858	1511
▲	Medium golden brown	611	898	2107
⊟	Golden brown	612	832	2108
◪	Medium antique violet	3041	870	0806
▣	Light antique violet	3042	869	0807
Ⅰ	Pale cream	822	390	1908
⋀	Medium beige grey	642	853	1906
⋂	Light beige grey	644	830	1907
◤	Sky blue	3752	976	1001
⊚	Silver grey	415	398	1803
Y	Yellow	744	301	0112
V	Apple green	368	261	1310
●	Clear green	3363	262	1311
⊞	Light clear green	3364	266	1501
Z	Medium salmon pink	760	9	0405
X	Light salmon pink	761	8	0404
⁄	Light shell pink	3713	48	0502
■	Dark grey	3022	392	1903
	White*	White	2	White

Note: bks house walls, door, roof and outer windows in dark grey;
use clear green for inner and outer border, and white (used for*
bks only) for window panes.

Garden Border Picture

What could be lovelier than a bed of
deep-scented hyacinths set against a
terrace wall, spilling over with delicate
pink and mauve aubrieta?
Add a background of golden yellow
forsythia and rose-coloured flowering
currant, and winter is soon forgotten.

GARDEN BORDER PICTURE

YOU WILL NEED

For the Garden Border Picture, mounted in a rectangular portrait frame, with an aperture measuring 22cm × 17cm (8¾in × 6¾in):

34cm × 30.5cm (13½in × 12in) of cream, 18-count Aida fabric
Stranded embroidery cotton in the colours given in the panel
No26 tapestry needle
Strong thread, for lacing across the back when mounting
Stiff cardboard for mounting
Frame of your choice

•

THE EMBROIDERY

Prepare the fabric, marking the centre lines of the design with basting stitches. Start your embroidery from the centre of the design, completing the cross stitching first, and then the backstitching. Use two strands of thread for both the cross stitch and the backstitch.

Gently steam press the finished embroidery on the wrong side.

ASSEMBLING THE PICTURE

Trim the edges of the embroidery until it measures 31cm × 26cm (12¼in × 10¼in) and centre the picture over the cardboard mount.

Lace the embroidery over the mount, following the instructions on page 13, and complete the assembly according to the manufacturer's instructions.

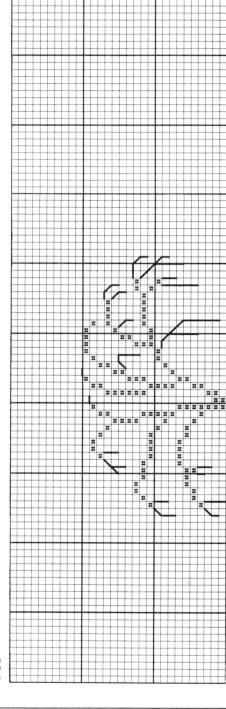

TOP

BORDER ▲		DMC	ANCHOR	MADEIRA			DMC	ANCHOR	MADEIRA
⊥	Dark grey	413	401	1713	▲	Dark blue	792	940	0905
∷	Grey	647	8581	1813	△	Blue	793	121	0906
•	Pale grey	648	900	1814	◩	Pale blue	794	175	0907
⊞	Brown	610	889	2106	⊞	Light reddish brown	356	5975	0402
▬	Reddish brown	355	341	0401	⊹	Pinkish brown	758	868	0403
╱	Pale lemon	746	275	0101	■	Dark green	3363	262	1602
ℤ	Yellowish brown	676	891	2208	⊡	Green	3364	260	1603
◥	Lemon	744	301	0112	÷	Lime green	472	264	1414
⊤	Dark mauve	552	101	0713	◆	Golden brown	435	365	2010
▢	Mauve	554	96	0711	⊟	Fawn	422	372	2102
◳	Pale mauve	211	342	0801	◸	Light golden brown	436	363	2011

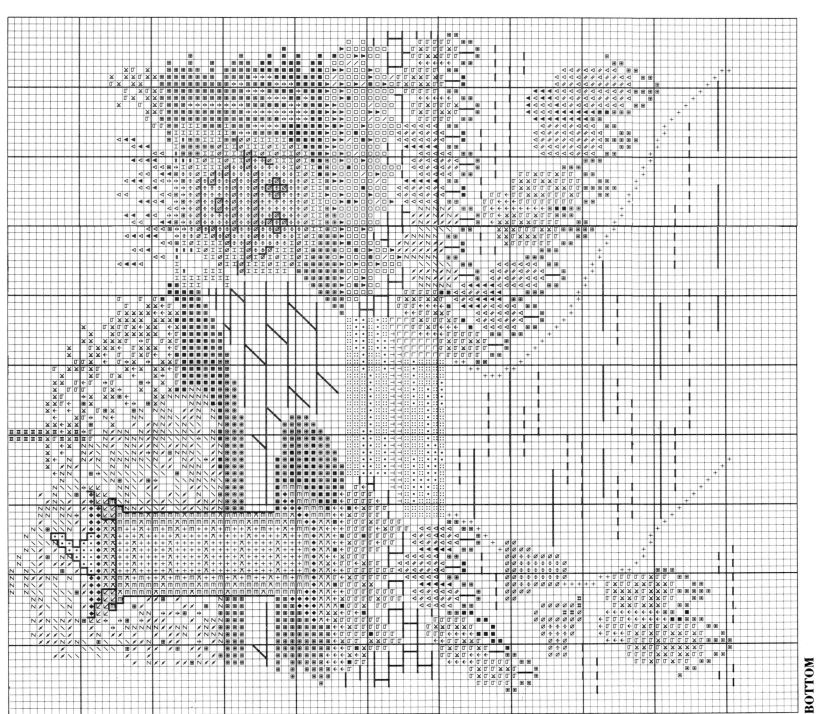

		DMC	ANCHOR	MADEIRA
◻	Brownish pink	3064	914	2312
+	Light fawn	738	942	2013
◹	Creamy fawn	739	885	2014
⊐	Silver grey	762	234	1804
↑	Deep pink	3607	87	0708
⊒	Pink	3608	86	0709
⊠	Pale pink	3609	85	0710

*Note: bks soil and tree twigs in brown, all paving slabs (front and
back paths) in light fawn, sundial and wall in grey, and terracotta
pot in reddish brown; the hyacinth stems are stitched in green and
dark green – green for the stems in the foreground, and dark green
for the background stems, as seen in the photograph.*

Vegetable Garden Sampler

An ideal gift for a gardener, this decorative sampler depicts the varied produce of a market garden. This project would provide a challenge for the more experienced cross stitcher.

VEGETABLE GARDEN SAMPLER

YOU WILL NEED

For the Vegetable Garden Sampler, mounted in a rectangular portrait frame with an aperture measuring 35cm × 31.5cm (14in × 12½in):

50cm x 50cm (20in x 20in) of antique white, 28-count evenweave fabric
Stranded embroidery cotton in the colours given in the panel
No24 tapestry needle
Strong thread, for lacing across the back
Stiff cardboard for mounting
Frame of your choice

•

THE EMBROIDERY

Prepare the fabric by marking the centre with lines of vertical and horizontal basting stitches and then mounting it in a hoop or frame as shown on page 9. Following the chart, start to embroider from the centre of the design, using two strands of cotton in the needle for cross stitches and french knots unless otherwise specified. Work the backstitch details using only one strand of cotton in the needle, unless otherwise specified. Refer to the diagram for how to work the three-quarter cross stitches. Gently steam press the finished embroidery on the wrong side.

ASSEMBLING THE PICTURE

Trim the edges of the embroidery and centre the picture over the cardboard mount. Lace the embroidery over the mount, following the instructions on page 13. Complete the assembly of the frame according to the manufacturer's instructions.

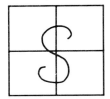

Where you see this

Stitch like this

●	Yellow	726
○	Terracotta	921
⬭	Pale green	471

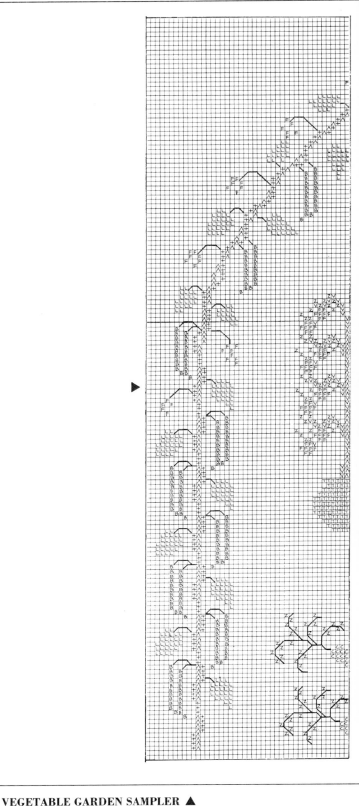

VEGETABLE GARDEN SAMPLER ▲				
		DMC	ANCHOR	MADEIRA
Λ	Brown	610	889	2106
+	Vine green	704	238	1308
B	Bean green	703	239	1307
L	Leaf green	702	226	1306
F	Red	349	13	0212
T	Orange	922	337	0310
Z	Deep green	3346	267	1407
R	Dark brown	840	379	1912

		DMC	ANCHOR	MADEIRA
V	Pale green	471	265	1501
N	Pale grey	415	398	1803
C	Terracotta	921	338	0311
	Yellow	726	295	0100
O	Blue	828	158	1101
·	White	White	White	White
	Dark grey	535	273	1809

Note: bks stems on bean arch in leaf green; the bunny tails in dark brown; the cauliflower in pale green (using two strands of cotton); the greenhouse (building) in dark grey; and the lettuce and stems on all greenhouse plants in deep green. Work french knots on yellow flowers in yellow, and bunny eyes in dark grey (using one strand of cotton).

FRUITS OF NATURE

If you're feeling fruity, there's a design in this chapter to suit. Bowlfuls of juicy grapes, apples, oranges, lemons and strawberries are just waiting to be stitched!

FRUITY CUSHION

For the Fruity Cushion, measuring
35cm (14in) square:

*45cm (18in) square of grey-blue, 28-count
evenweave fabric
Stranded embroidery cotton in the colours
given in the panel
No24 tapestry needle
Matching sewing thread
45cm (18in) square plain or patterned fabric, for
cushion back
35cm (14in) square cushion pad
2m (2¼yd) pearl grey silk cushion cord, 6mm (¼in)
in diameter*

•

THE EMBROIDERY

Prepare the fabric, marking the centre with
horizontal and vertical lines of basting stitches, and
mount it in a hoop as shown on page 9. Following
the chart, start to embroider from the centre of the
design, using two strands of cotton in the needle for
cross stitches (except for the gold thread where you
need only one strand), and working over two threads
of fabric in each direction. Work the backstitch
details using one strand of cotton in the needle.
Gently steam press the finished embroidery on the
wrong side.

MAKING UP THE COVER

Keeping the design centred, trim the fabric to
measure 37cm (14³⁄₄in). Machine zigzag stitch the
raw edges to prevent fraying. With right sides
together, stitch the front and back pieces of the
cushion cover together, taking a 1.5cm (⁵⁄₈in) seam
allowance, and leaving an opening of 23cm (9¼in)
on one side. Turn the cover right side out and press.
Insert the cushion pad and slip stitch the opening
closed. Trim the edge of the cushion with the
cushion cord, making a 13cm (5½in) loop at each
corner, and slip stitch it in place.

For a fuller cushion, reduce the size of the cover
by 1.5cm (⁵⁄₈in) all around.

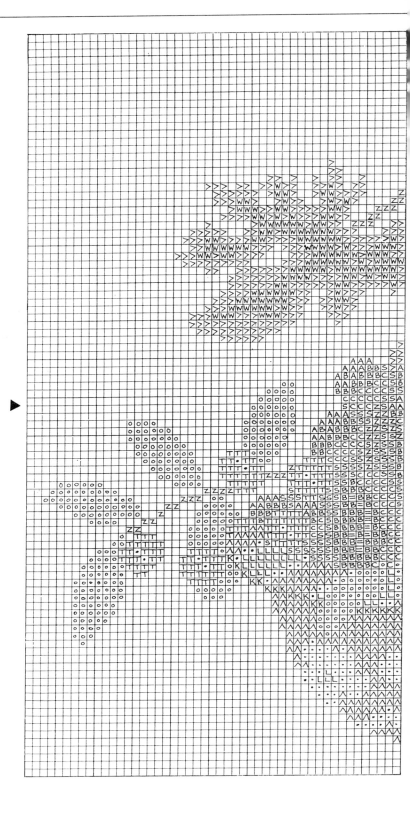

FRUITY CUSHION ▲	DMC	ANCHOR	MADEIRA
• White	White	White	White
Λ Pale blue	813	0160	1019
L Deep blue	312	0979	1005
C Dark purple	552	0100	0713
B Medium purple	553	098	0712
A Light purple	554	096	0711
T Red	321	013	0510
S Very dark purple	550	0101	0714
□ Deep grey	3799	236	1713
Z Brown	869	0944	2105

	DMC	ANCHOR	MADEIRA
V Old gold	734	279	1610
■ Dark old gold	832	0907	2202
> Avocado green	470	0266	1502
W Dark avocado green	469	0267	1503
D Pale green	989	0256	1401
P Mid green	988	0257	1402
O Dark green	987	0258	1403
K Light gold (metallic)	ART.282		

Note: bks the stems in dark green.

Autumn Harvest Tray

The fruits of autumn in all their abundance and rich colourings are vividly portrayed on this stitched piece, which has been made up in the form of a tray. Used throughout the year, it reminds us of earth's bounty and blessings.

AUTUMN HARVEST TRAY

For the Tray, measuring 24cm (9½in) square:

37.5cm (15in) square of 14-count,
Fiddler's Lite Aida fabric
Stranded embroidery cotton in the colours
given in the panel
No24 tapestry needle
Wooden tray (for suppliers, see page 220)

•

THE EMBROIDERY

Prepare the fabric as described on page 9; find the centre by folding, and mark the horizontal and vertical centre lines with basting stitches in a light-coloured thread. Set the fabric in a frame or hoop and count out from the centre to start stitching at a point convenient to you.

Two threads of cotton were used in the needle for cross stitches and one for backstitching. Work all cross stitches first, taking them over one block of fabric. Make sure that all top stitches run in the same direction. Finally, work all backstitch details.

Remove the embroidery from the frame, and, if necessary, wash gently and then steam press on the wrong side. Do not remove the basting stitches at this stage.

ASSEMBLING THE TRAY

Using a soft pencil, mark the mounting card supplied with the tray horizontally and vertically across the centre. Place the embroidery face down with the card on top, basting and pencil lines matching.

Fold the fabric over at each corner, securing it with masking tape. Working on one side and then the opposite side, fold over the edges of the fabric on all sides and secure with pieces of masking tape. Check to see that the embroidery is centred; if not, simply release the masking tape and readjust the position. Neaten the corners by folding them over to form a mitre (see page 12) and secure with masking tape. Carefully remove basting stitches.

Insert the mounted embroidery into the tray, using the glass and backing boards provided and following the manufacturer's instructions.

AUTUMN HARVEST ▶		DMC	ANCHOR	MADEIRA
X	Light grey green	523	859	1512
●	Pink red	3328	1024	0406
P	Medium salmon pink	760	9	0405
/	Light salmon pink	761	8	0404
G	Clear green	3363	262	1602
	Dark tan brown*	433	359	2304
O	Medium tan brown	435	371	2303
T	Light tan brown	437	362	2012
L	Medium gold	676	891	2208
M	Medium purple	553	98	0712
−	Light purple	554	96	0711
▲	Dark yellow green	3051	681	1508
I	Light straw	3047	852	2205
S	Medium straw	3046	887	2206
U	Khaki green	370	855	2112
A	Apple green	368	261	1310
B	Medium golden brown	612	832	2108
C	Medium orange	722	323	0307
\	Light orange	402	1047	2307
Y	Medium yellow	744	301	0112
•	Light gold	677	886	2205
■	Dark tan	420	374	2104

Note: bks the basket outline, the fruit stems and wheatsheaf in dark tan brown (used for backstitch only) and the outer line and flourishes in clear green.*

Strawberry Garland Table Set

Perfect for a summer lunch party, the twining strawberry design of this table set adds a touch of distinction to a plain tablecloth, while the matching serviette holders complete the fruity look.

STRAWBERRY GARLAND TABLE SET

YOU WILL NEED

For the Tablecloth, measuring 103cm (41¼in) square:

1m (40in) square of pink, 25-count evenweave fabric
Matching sewing thread
Stranded embroidery cotton in the colours given in the panel
No24 tapestry needle
425cm (170in) white lace, 2cm (¾in) wide, for edging

For the Serviette Holders, each measuring 4.5cm × 4.5cm (1¾in × 1¾in):

Oddments of white, 18-count Aida fabric
Stranded embroidery cotton in the colours given in the panel
No24 tapestry needle
Serviette holders (for suppliers, see page 220)

●

THE TABLECLOTH

Prepare the fabric by machine zigzag stitching around the edges to prevent it fraying. Mark the centre of the fabric with lines of horizontal and vertical basting stitches and mount the fabric in a hoop or frame as shown on page 9. Following the chart, start to embroider from the centre of the design, marked M on the garland chart, using two strands of cotton in the needle and working over two threads of the fabric. Work the lower half of the garland first, then turn the fabric around through 180 degrees and complete the central design.

To position the corner motifs, baste diagonal lines outwards from the centre of the fabric. Count 100 stitches (200 threads of the fabric) from the outer edge of the garland to the letter C on the corner motif chart. Work the right hand motif first, then turn the chart 90 degrees clockwise, and position for the left hand corner in the same way. To embroider the remaining two corners, turn the fabric around through 180 degrees and repeat. Gently steam press the finished embroidery on the wrong side.

To finish the tablecloth, machine stitch white lace around the edges, making pleats at each corner.

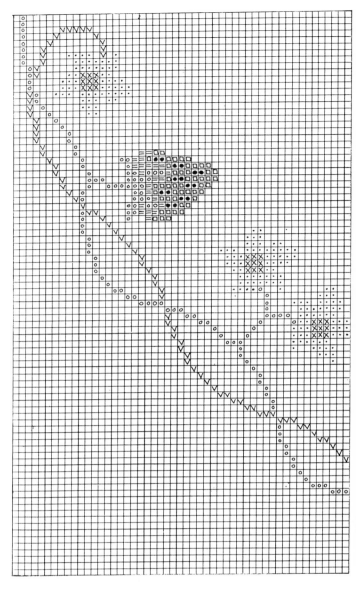

THE SERVIETTE HOLDERS

Mark the centre of each oddment of fabric with basting stitches and mount the fabric in a hoop or frame (see page 9). Following the chart, embroider the motif, starting from the centre of the design and using one strand of cotton in the needle. Steam press the finished embroidery on the wrong side.

Trim the fabric to fit the serviette holder and slide it gently in position in the holder. Repeat to make the required number of serviette holders.

STRAWBERRY GARLAND TABLE SET ▲		DMC	ANCHOR	MADEIRA
·	White	White	White	White
V	Pale green	417	0265	1501
O	Dark green	3346	0267	1407
●	Pale yellow	744	0301	0112
X	Deep yellow	744	0305	0113
□	Red	321	013	0510
=	Deep red	498	047	0510

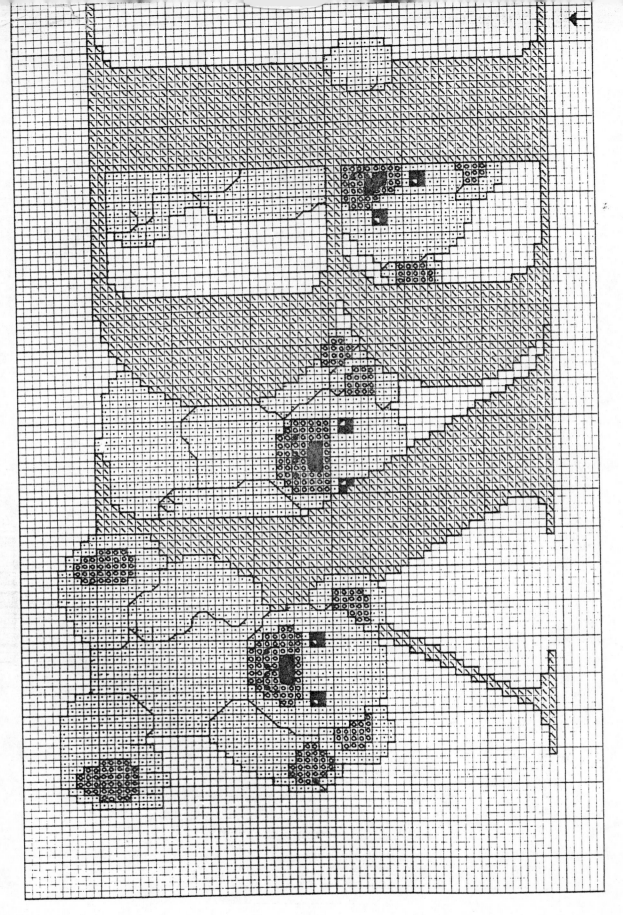

with dark baby blue _ or pale dusty rose with dark dusty rose
(starred colours are used for backstitching only); use either baby
blues (for a boy) or dusty pinks (for a girl); two skeins needed
of tan, and three of either baby blue or pale dusty rose.

◄ DMC	ANCHOR	MADEIRA
White	2	White
321	47	0510
815	43	0513
3325	159	1002
311	148	1006
322	978	1004
3047	886	2205
782	307	2212
436	363	2011
801	357	2007*
310	403	Black

to backstitch around bodies, dark baby blue navy for other clothing.

MOTHER AND DAUGHTER ▼		DMC	ANCHOR	MAD
□	White	White	2	W
/	Pink	3326	26	0
•	Dark pink	335	42	0
C	Medium lavender	210	104	0
II	Dark lavender	208	110	0
O	Pale golden wheat	3047	886	2
·	Tan	436	363	2
	Dark coffee*	801	357	20
	Light grey*	415	398	1
■	Black	310	403	B

Note: dark coffee* used to backstitch around bodies, light
sleeve.

For each Cushion, measuring 25cm (10in) square, excluding lace edging:

35cm (14in) square of white, 14-count Aida fabric
27.5cm (11in) square of contrast fabric,
to back your cushion
2.4m (2⅔yds) of white lace edging,
4cm (1½in) deep
Stranded embroidery cotton in the colours given
in the appropriate panel
Matching sewing thread
No24 tapestry needle
27.5cm (11in) square cushion pad

cross stitching, starting a
strands in the needle th
main areas first, and th
stitching, this time usin,
needle. Steam press on the

MAKING UP

Trim the embroidery to
square. Using a tiny fre
edges of the lace together
close to the straight edge;
and, with the right side of
the lace lying on the fabri

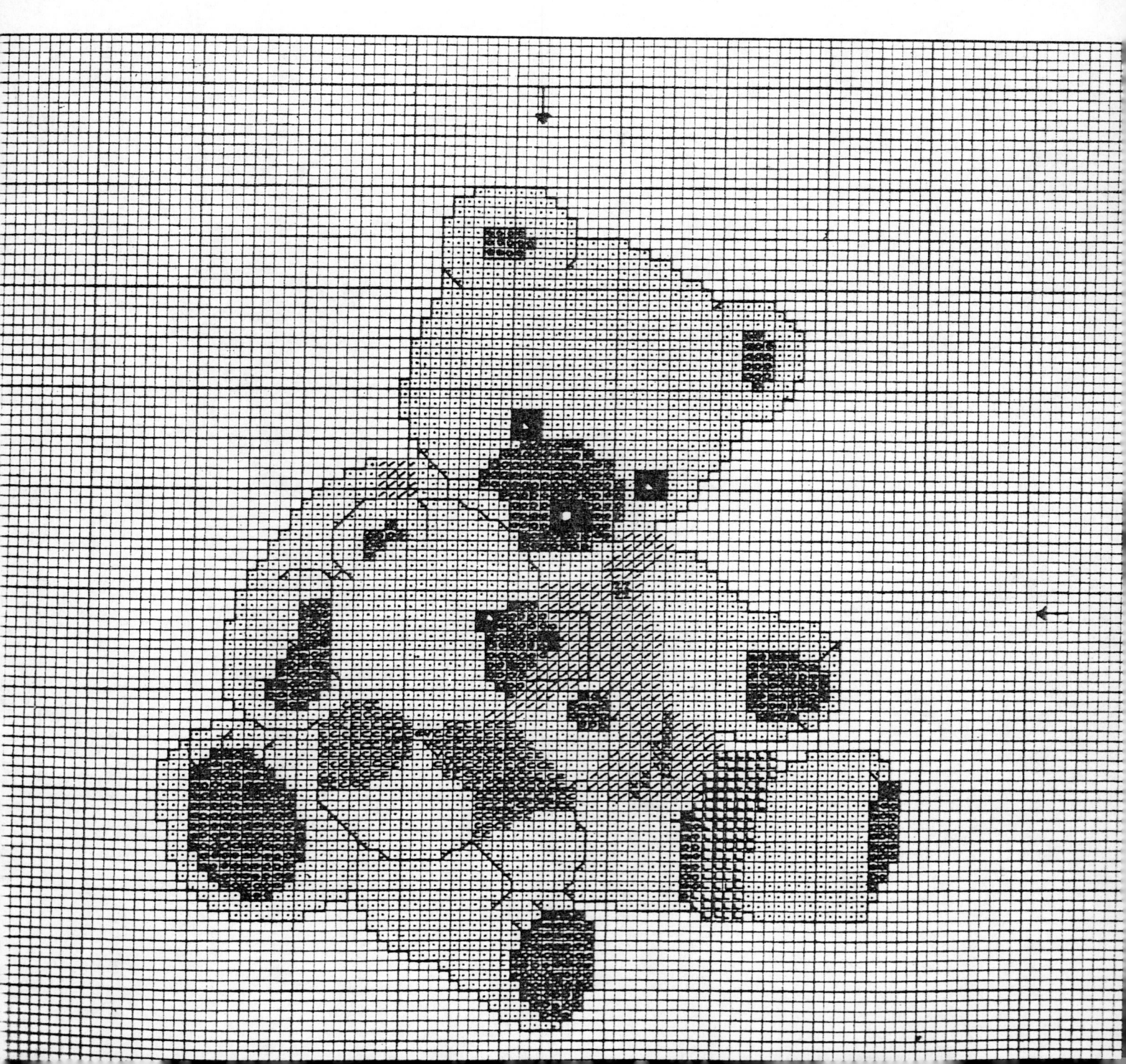

A PICTURE FOR BABY

YOU WILL NEED

For the Picture, measuring 50cm × 24cm (20in × 9½), unframed:

58.5cm × 31.5cm (23in × 12½in) of white, 14-count Aida fabric

Stranded embroidery cotton in the colours given in the panel; two skeins of tan are required, and three of either baby blue or pale dusty rose

50cm × 24cm (20in × 9½in) of firm cardboard, for a mount

50cm × 24cm (20in × 9½in) of iron-on interfacing (optional – see Mounting the picture)

No24 tapestry needle

Picture frame of your choice

THE EMBROIDERY

Prepare the fabric, marking the centre lines of the design with basting stitches, and mount it in a frame, following the instructions on page 7. Referring to the chart, complete the cross stitching, using three strands in the needle throughout. Embroider the main areas first, and then finish with the backstitching, this time using two strands of thread in the needle. If necessary, steam press on the wrong side.

It is a good idea to leave the basting stitches in at this stage, as they will prove useful in helping to centre your design on the mount.

MOUNTING THE PICTURE

Take care that your working surface is absolutely clean and dry. If you wish to use an iron-on interfacing, to help to avoid wrinkles, iron this to the back of the embroidery, following the same procedure as for the cards on page 176. If you are not using interfacing, leave the basting stitches in place and remove them after mounting.

Mount your picture on the firm cardboard, following the instructions given for heavier fabrics. Mark the centre of the board at the top, bottom and sides, and match centre marks for accurate alignment.

A PICTURE FOR BABY

YOU WILL NEED

For the Picture, measuring 50cm × 24cm
(20in × 9½), unframed:

58.5cm × 31.5cm (23in × 12½in) of white,
14-count Aida fabric
Stranded embroidery cotton in the colours given
in the panel; two skeins of tan are required, and
three of either baby blue or pale dusty rose
50cm × 24cm (20in × 9½in) of firm cardboard,
for a mount
50cm × 24cm (20in × 9½in) of iron-on
interfacing (optional — see Mounting the picture)
No24 tapestry needle
Picture frame of your choice

THE EMBROIDERY

Prepare the fabric, marking the centre lines of the
design with basting stitches, and mount it in a

using three strands in the
Embroider the main areas first, and t
the backstitching, this time using
thread in the needle. If necessary, s
the wrong side.

It is a good idea to leave the bastin
this stage, as they will prove usefu
centre your design on the mount.

MOUNTING THE PICTU

Take care that your working surfac
clean and dry. If you wish to use a
facing, to help to avoid wrinkles, iron
of the embroidery, following the sam
for the cards on page 176. If you are
facing, leave the basting stitches
remove them after mounting.
Mount your picture on the firm ca
ing the instructions given for heavi
the centre of the board at the top, b
and match centre marks for accurat

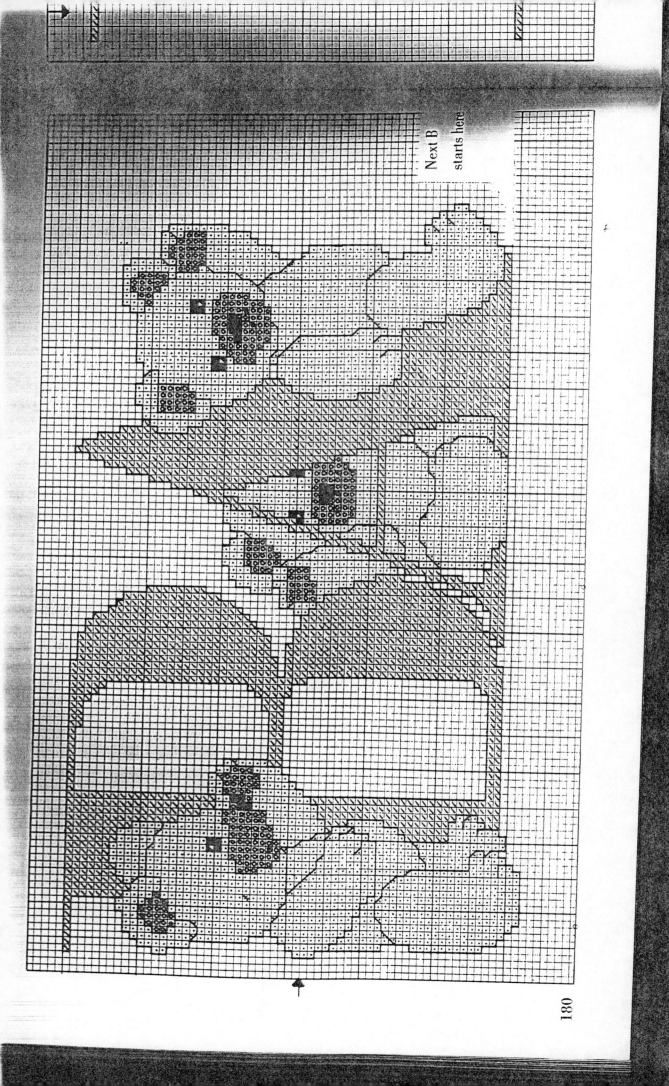

Next B
starts here

the centre of the board at the top, bottom and sides, and match centre marks for accurate alignment.

design with basting stitches, and mount it in a

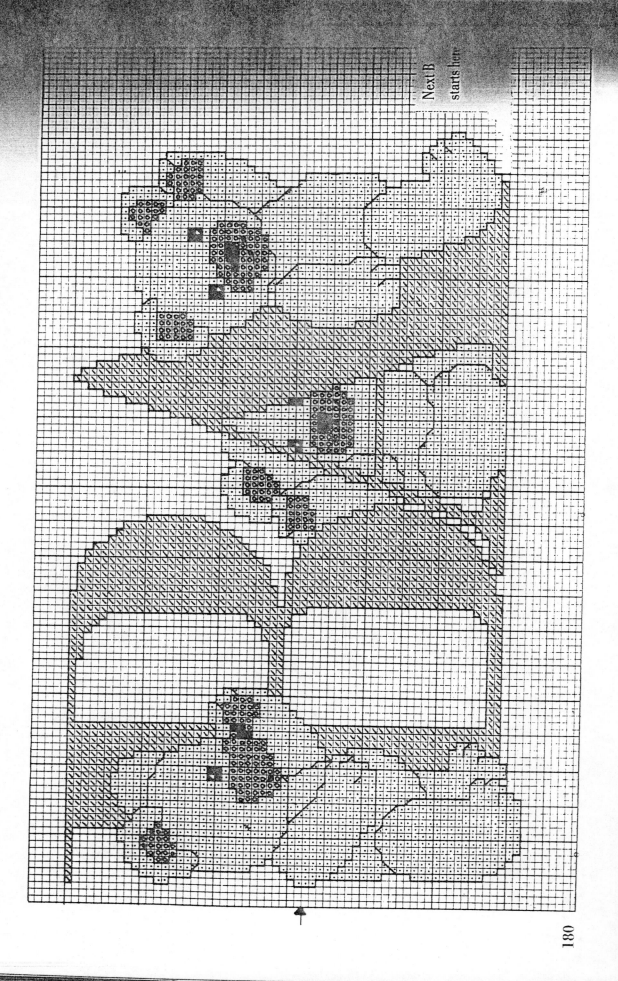

Next B
starts here

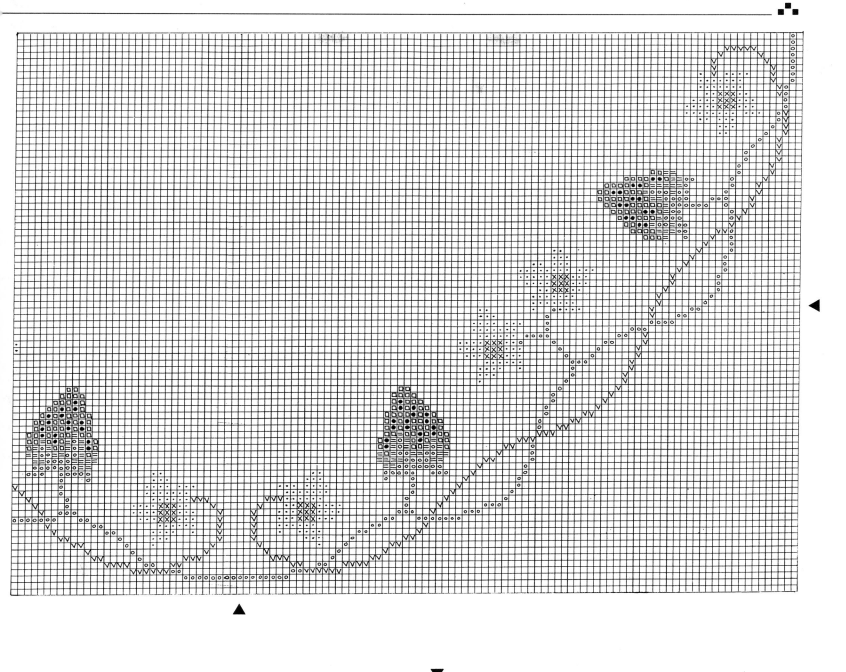
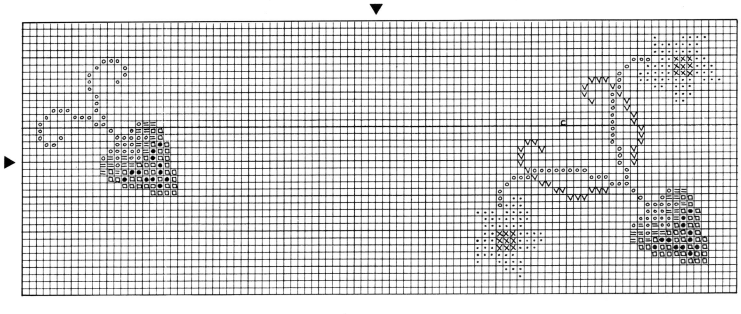

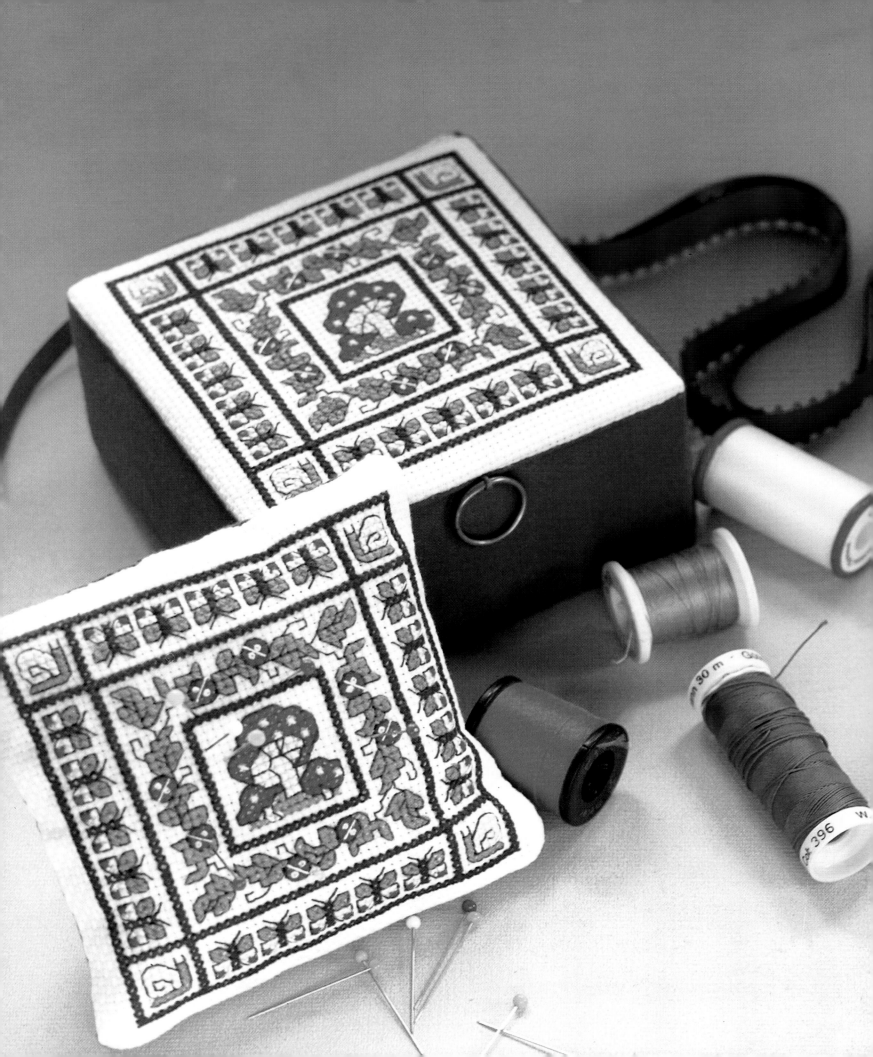

Woodland Magic

Ladybirds, butterflies, snails and toadstools create a simple square design that can be adapted to a multitude of uses. A pincushion, needlecase and box are shown here, but the design would also make a charming birthday card, while either the outer or inner border, or both, could be used for a picture frame.

WOODLAND MAGIC

For the Pincushion, measuring
10cm (4in) square:

20cm (8in) square of white, 14-count Aida fabric
12.5cm (5in) square of green cotton fabric,
for backing
Stranded embroidery cotton in the colours
given in the panel
No26 tapestry needle
Wool, kapok or polyester filling

For the Needlecase, measuring
10cm (4in) square:

30cm × 20cm (12 × 8in) of white,
14-count Aida fabric
24cm × 12.5cm (9½ × 5in) of green backing fabric
20cm × 10cm (8in × 4in) of green felt
Stranded embroidery cotton in the colours given
in the panel
No26 tapestry needle

For the Box, 5cm (2in) deep, with a top measuring
10cm (4in) square:

20cm (8in) square of white, 14-count Aida fabric
Stranded embroidery cotton in the colours given
in the panel
No26 tapestry needle
Seven pieces of green cotton fabric,
each 12.5cm (5in) square
Stiff card (medium thickness) – four pieces
5cm × 10cm (2in × 4in),
and four pieces 10cm (4in) square
Lightweight polyester wadding –
four pieces 5cm × 10cm (2in × 4in),
and one piece 10cm (4in) square
25cm (10in) of thin white cord
Small brass curtain ring
Glue stick
Masking tape
Strong thread, for lacing across the back

•

THE EMBROIDERY

For either the pincushion or the box, start by preparing the fabric as described on page 9; find the centre either by folding the fabric in half and then in half again, and lightly pressing the folded corner, or by marking the horizontal and vertical centre lines with basting stitches in a light-coloured thread. Mount the fabric in a hoop (see page 9) and start the design from the centre.

If you are making the needlecase, start by folding the fabric in half and half again, to find the centre and then baste a rectangle measuring 21.5cm × 10cm (8½in × 4in) around the centre of the fabric. On the right-hand half of the rectangle (the front of the needlecase) mark the centre of this half only with horizontal and vertical lines of basting stitches in a light coloured thread. This centre is the centre of the design.

Following the chart and working from the centre outwards, complete all the cross stitching first, using two strands of thread in the needle. Finish with the backstitching, again using two strands of thread. Remove the finished embroidery from the hoop and wash if necessary, then press lightly on the wrong side, using a steam iron.

PINCUSHION

Keeping the design centred, trim the Aida to measure 12.5cm (5in) square. Remove basting stitches. Place the embroidery and backing fabric right sides together and stitch around the sides, taking a 12mm (½in) seam allowance and leaving a small gap in one side for the filling. Trim across the seam allowance at the corners; turn the pincushion right side out and fill tightly. Slipstitch across the opening.

NEEDLECASE

Trim the embroidery fabric, leaving a 12mm (½in) seam allowance around the basted rectangle. Remove basting stitches. Place the embroidery and backing fabric with right sides together and stitch around the edge, taking a 12mm (½in) seam allowance and leaving a small gap, for turning, on the lower edge at the blank half of the fabric. Trim across the seam allowance at the corners; turn the fabric right side out and slipstitch the gap. Using pinking shears, trim the felt to fit inside the needlecase, then attach it inside the centre fold, using small running stitches.

BOX

To prepare the side sections, first glue a piece of batting to one side of the each of the four 5cm × 10cm (2in × 4in) pieces of card. For each side, take a piece of green fabric and lay a card piece, padded side down, on the wrong side of the fabric, with an allowance of 12mm (½in) of fabric showing at each side, and a scant 15mm (⅝in) showing at the bottom edge. Fold in the sides and tape them, as shown. Bring the lower edge of the fabric up over the card; turn under a 12mm (½in) allowance along the top edge and bring it down to cover the lower raw edge of fabric. Stitch along the lower edge, so that the stitching line is just slightly to the back of the card, not along the bottom. Oversewing the edges with neat stitches, join the four sides of the box together to make a square, with the stitched lower edges facing inwards.

Take three square sections (base and inside lid) and cover one side of each with a piece of fabric: mitre the corners and fold in the sides, holding them with tape (see page 12). With the fabric outside, gently push one base section into the prepared side piece and neatly oversew the bottom edge on all sides. Turn the box over and neatly stitch white cord along the top edge of one side (now the back edge), allowing the ends to run down the inside corners and onto the base. Push the second base piece, fabric

side up, into the box covering the cord ends and the back of the first base section.

Keeping the design centred, trim the embroidery to measure 12.5cm (5in) square, and remove basting stitches. Glue wadding to one side of the remaining uncovered piece of card, and lace the work over the padded card (see page 13). Place the two lid sections with wrong sides together and neatly oversew the edges. Stitch the lid to the cord at the back of the box, and stitch the brass ring to the front centre edge of the lid.

WOODLAND MAGIC ▼	ANCHOR	DMC	MADEIRA
☐ Leaf green	226	702	1306
● Brown	352	300	2304
· Lemon	292	746	101
☒ Red	47	304	511
Dark green*	228	700	1304

Note: bks butterfly feelers, snail shells and toadstools in brown, butterfly wings, ladybirds, leaves and snail bodies in dark green* (used for bks only), and the central line down the ladybirds in lemon. Make one french knot on each side of the central line down the ladybirds, using two strands of lemon.

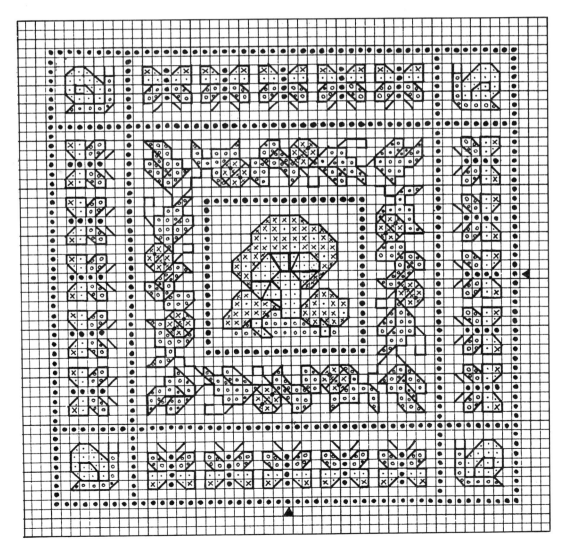

Apple Trellis Bag

This stylish cross stitch design features a pattern of apples surrounded by a trellis latticework. The bag can be used as a clutch bag or purse, or even a make-up bag.

APPLE TRELLIS BAG

YOU WILL NEED

For the Apple Trellis Bag, measuring
21.5cm × 14.5cm (8¼in × 5¾in):

Two pieces 32cm × 56cm (12¾in × 22⅜in)
mushroom, 28-count evenweave fabric
Stranded embroidery cotton in the colours
given in the panel
No24 tapestry needle
32cm × 56cm (12¾in × 22⅜in) medium-weight
iron-on interfacing
Matching sewing thread
Popper fastener

•

THE EMBROIDERY

Prepare the fabric by marking the outline and centre
of the design area with basting stitches (see the
diagram), and then mounting the fabric in a hoop as
shown on page 9. Following the chart, start to
embroider from the centre of the design panel using
two strands of cotton in the needle. Gently steam
press the finished embroidery on the wrong side.

MAKING UP THE BAG

Iron the interfacing onto the wrong side of the
embroidered panel. Trim both fabric rectangles so
that they measure 24cm × 47cm (9½in × 18¾in).
Machine zigzag stitch around all sides of both fabric
rectangles. With right sides together, sew the
rectangles together around three sides, leaving one
short side open, and press. Turn right side out and
press again. Turn raw edges under and slip stitch
the remaining open edge closed, and press. Fold the
bag into its finished shape and slip stitch the side
seams together along the outer edge of the seams.
Place the popper fastener on the inside front of the
flap and front panel, and stitch in place.

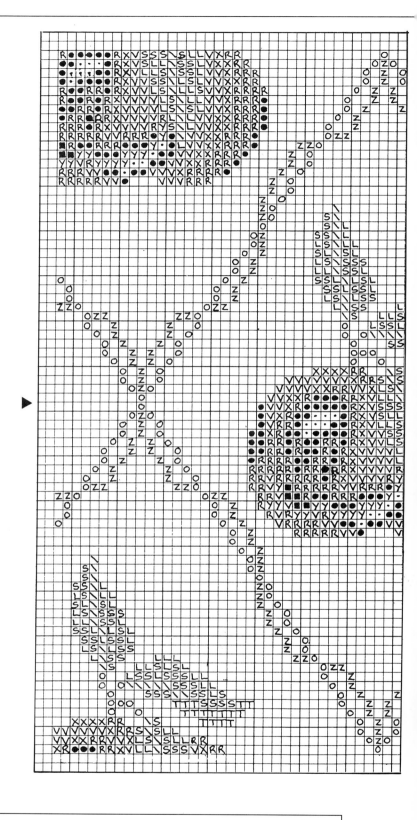

APPLE TRELLIS BAG ▶	DMC	ANCHOR	MADEIRA		DMC	ANCHOR	MADEIRA
O Brown	610	889	2106	V Brownish red	3779	868	403
\ Darkest green	936	846	1507	X Crimson	304	47	0509
S Dark green	469	267	1503	R Red	349	13	0212
L Medium green	470	266	1502	● Salmon pink	350	11	0213
T Light green	471	265	1501	· Light salmon pink	351	10	0214
■ Dark brown	3031	360	2003	Z Drab green	3011	845	1607
Y Yellow	743	305	0113				

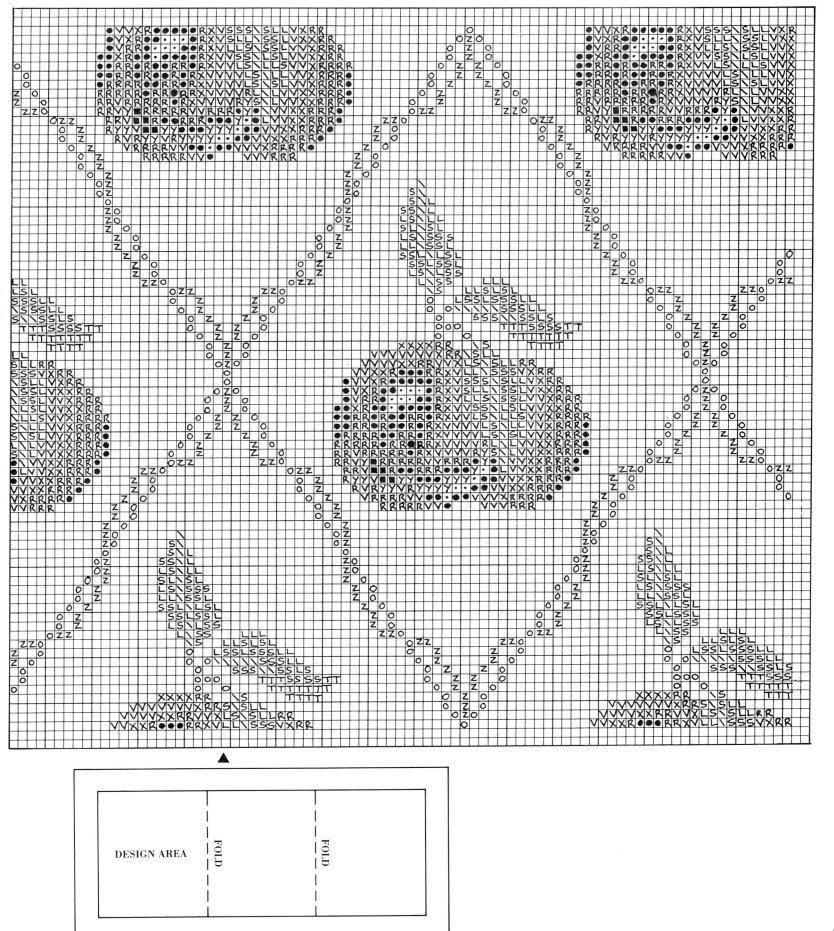

DESIGN AREA | FOLD | FOLD

Framed Fruits

The briar rose, also known as
eglantine, is a fragrant wild hedgerow
rose, much pinker than the common
dog rose. In the autumn it bears shiny
red hips, rich in vitamin C.
The bramble is also a member of the
rose family, with white or pale pink
flowers in early summer, giving way to
a profusion of ripened berries
later in the year.

FRAMED FRUITS

YOU WILL NEED

For each Picture, set in a frame with a picture area measuring 18cm × 12.5cm (7in × 5in):

27cm × 23cm (10¾in × 9in) of eau-de-Nil Aida fabric, with 18 threads to 2.5cm (1in)
Stranded embroidery cotton in the colours given in the panel
No26 tapestry needle
Strong thread, for lacing across the back
Cross-over frame (for suppliers, see page 220)

•

THE EMBROIDERY

For each picture, prepare the fabric, marking the centre lines of the design with basting stitches, and set it in a frame (see page 9). Start your embroidery from the centre of the design, completing the main areas first, and then the backstitching. Use two strands of thread for both the cross stitch and backstitching, except for fine details, such as the stamens, where one thread is recommended.

Gently steam press the finished embroidery on the wrong side. It is helpful to retain the central basting stitches at this stage.

ASSEMBLING THE PICTURES

Each picture is assembled in the same way. Trim the edges of the embroidery until it measures 23cm × 18cm (9in × 7¼in). Mark the central horizontal and vertical lines on the mount provided and, matching these with the central basting stitches, lace the embroidery over the mount, following the instructions on page 13. Carefully remove the basting stitches.

Complete the assembly according to the manufacturer's instructions.

BRIAR ROSE ◄	DMC	ANCHOR	MADEIRA
╷ White	White	2	White
· Cream	712	590	2101
⊤ Palest pink	3689	49	0607
I Pale pink	605	60	0613
⋰ Pink	604	66	0614
+ Deep pink	603	62	0701
⊣ Lemon	744	301	0112
⋱ Yellow	743	297	0113
◢ Bright yellow	972	298	0107
x Orange	970	316	0204
∐ Deep orange	900	333	0208
⋮─ Green	3347	266	1408
⊥ Medium green	3346	817	1407
⊤ Dark green	3345	268	1406
— Yellowish green	472	264	1414
Dark yellowish green*	470	267	1503
⌟ Fawn	729	890	2209
⅃ Yellowish brown	831	889	2201

Note: bks rosehips in dark yellowish green*, stamens in yellow, pollen tips on stamens, adjacent flower centre and dying leaf in yellowish brown, leaf stalks in dark green, and rosehip stalks in medium green.

BRAMBLE ▼	DMC	ANCHOR	MADEIRA
· White	White	2	White
╱ Soft pink	819	271	0501
╷ Pink	3688	66	0605
⊤ Deep pink	3350	42	0603
— Pale mauve	3609	85	0710
x Purplish pink	3608	86	0709
⊐ Navy	939	152	1009
⋮─ Pale green	3013	842	1605
I Green	3363	262	1602
+ Dark green	520	862	1514
⌟ Yellowish green	3348	264	1409
⋰ Greyish green	3052	859	1509
⊣ Ginger brown	433	371	2008
∐ Dark brown	3031	905	2003
⊥ Dark grey	413	401	1713
■ Black	310	403	Black

Note: bks base of new fruit in ginger brown, tips of stamens and base of flowers in dark green, stamens in pale green and all stems in yellowish green.

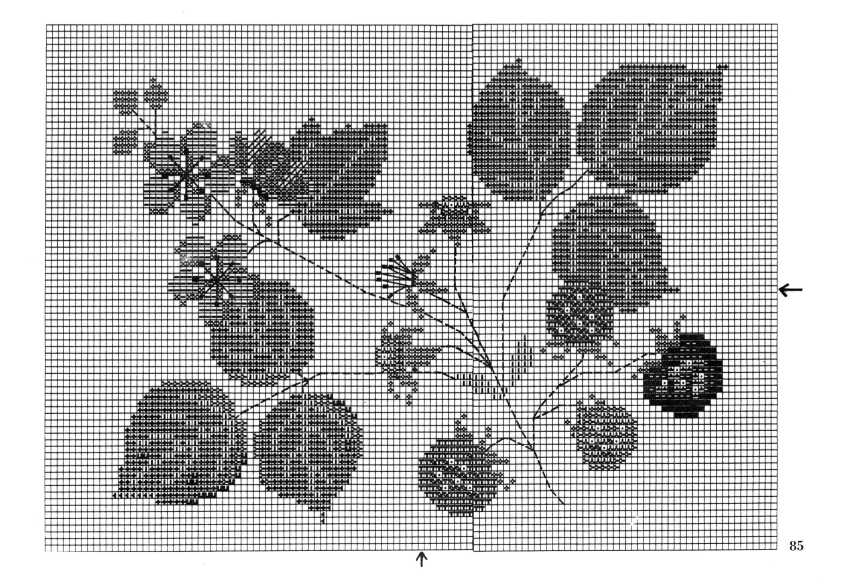

Citrus Kitchen Towel

Add a touch of zest to your washing up with this kitchen towel decorated with lemons and limes. This project is quick and easy to stitch and would be ideal for beginners.

CITRUS KITCHEN TOWEL

YOU WILL NEED

For the Citrus Kitchen Towel, measuring
66.5cm × 50cm (26½in × 20in):

*Kitchen towel with two 9.5cm × 52.5cm
(3¼in × 21in) white, 8-count Aida panels with red
edging (for suppliers, see page 220)
Stranded embroidery cotton in the colours given in
the panel
No24 tapestry needle
White sewing thread*

THE EMBROIDERY

Prepare the towel by machine zigzag stitching
around the raw edges to prevent fraying. Mark the
centre of each panel with lines of horizontal and
vertical basting stitches and mount in a hoop or
frame as shown on page 9.

Following the chart and working on one panel of
the towel at a time, start to embroider from the
centre of the design, using four strands of cotton in
the needle. Gently steam press the finished
embroidery on the wrong side.

FINISHING THE TOWEL

Turn under a 12mm (½in) hem around all the edges
of the towel and then machine stitch using white
sewing thread.

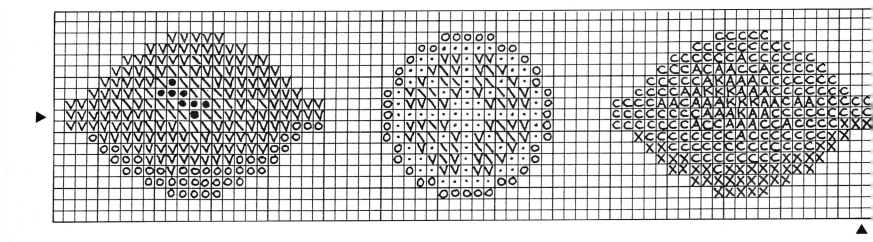

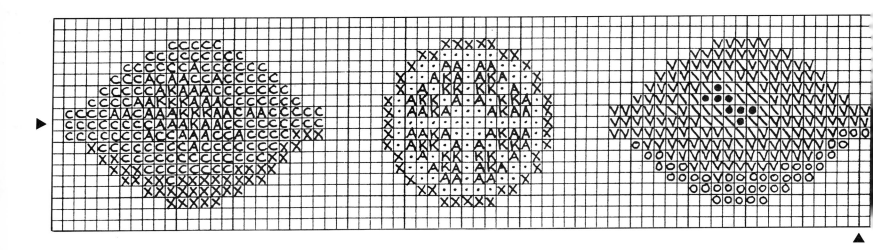

CITRUS KITCHEN TOWEL ▼	DMC	ANCHOR	MADEIRA
• Ecru	Ecru	387	Ecru
X Darkest green	987	244	1403
C Green	988	243	1402
A Pale green	3348	264	1409
K Palest green	472	278	1414
V Yellow	726	295	0100
O Darkest yellow	725	306	0108
\ Pale yellow	727	293	0110
● Palest yellow	3078	292	0102

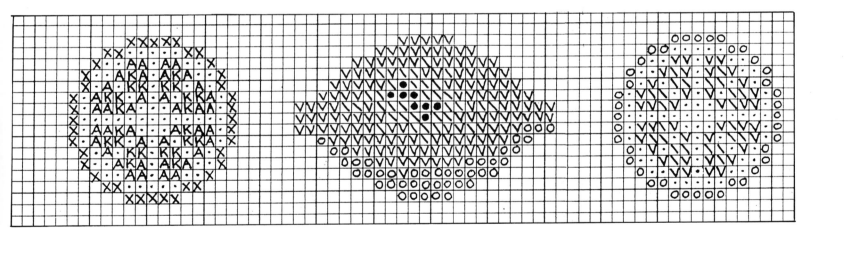

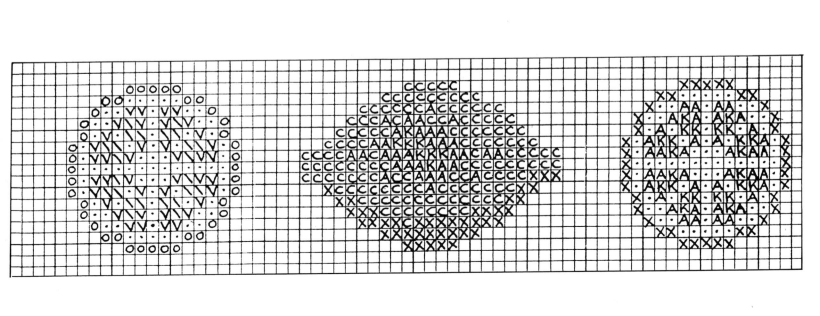

FABULOUS FLOWERS

Flowers are one of the greatest joys of nature and there are few pleasures to equal that of creating a garden filled with beautiful flowers. In this chapter the delicate enchantment of wild flowers and the beauty of garden flowers have been translated into charming cross stitch designs.

Rosa xanthina
Rosa farreri persetosa
Rosa spinosissima
Rosa rugosa

BOTANICAL SAMPLER

YOU WILL NEED

For the Sampler, with a design area measuring
17cm × 23.5cm (6¾in × 9½in), or 103 stitches
by 133 stitches, here in a frame measuring
27.5cm × 33cm (11in × 13in):

*27cm × 33.5cm (10¾in × 13¼in) of cream
14-count Aida fabric
Stranded embroidery cotton in the colours given
in the panel
No24 tapestry needle
Strong thread, for lacing across the back
Cardboard, for mounting, sufficient to fit into the
frame recess
Frame of your choice*

●

THE EMBROIDERY

Prepare the fabric and stretch it in a frame as
explained on page 9. Following the chart, start the
embroidery at the centre of the design, using two
strands of embroidery cotton in the needle. Work
each stitch over one block of fabric in each
direction. Make sure that all the top crosses run in
the same direction and that each row is worked into
the same holes as the top or bottom of the row
before, leaving no spaces between the rows.

Make french knots for seeds in the bottom left-
hand corner with six and three strands of light and
medium green stranded cotton respectively, winding the cotton once around the needle and using the
picture as a guide. Make the straight lines in backstitch with three strands of light green cotton.

Work the names around the outside in backstitch
using two strands of dark brown cotton, and the
branches with two strands of medium brown cotton.

MAKING UP

Gently steam press the work on the wrong side and
mount as explained on page 13. Set your finished
sampler in a traditional frame.

BOTANICAL SAMPLER ▶		DMC	ANCHOR	MADEIRA
‡	Light pink	605	50	0613
╱	Medium pink	604	60	0614
r	Dark pink	603	62	0701
e	Darkest pink	602	63	0702
−	Light mauve	210	108	0803
❭	Medium mauve	208	111	0804
s	Dark mauve	550	101	0714
%	Light yellow	3078	292	0102
a	Medium yellow	743	301	0113
o	Dark yellow	742	302	0107
c	Light green	3348	264	1409
x	Medium green	3347	266	1408
=	Dark green	937	268	1504
s	Light brown	640	393	1905
╲	Medium brown	841	378	1911
	Dark brown*	938	381	2005

* Used for bks writing.

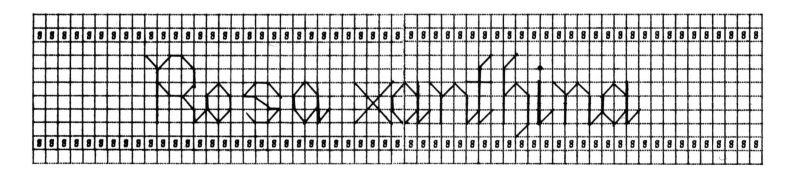

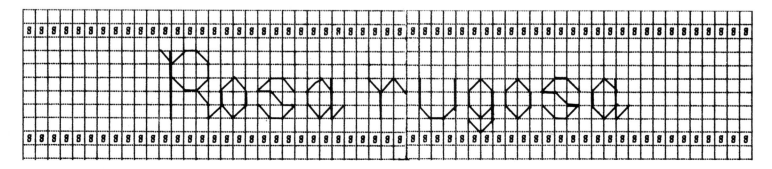

Foxglove Duo

This beautiful cushion would enhance any sitting room, and to add that extra dimension, why not complement it with an elegant wall hanger?

FOXGLOVE DUO

YOU WILL NEED

For the Foxglove Cushion Cover, measuring 47cm (18½in) square:

52cm (21in) of cream Aida fabric, with 14 threads to 2.5cm (1in)
48.5cm (19½in) square of furnishing fabric, for the cushion back
Two 48.5cm (19½in) squares of strong unbleached cotton fabric, for the inner cover
Stranded embroidery cotton in the colours given in the panel
No24 tapestry needle
3m (3½yds) of matching green (or deep pink) cushion cord, 6mm (¼in) in diameter
47cm (18½in) cushion pad

For the Wall Hanging, measuring 41cm × 16.5cm (16½in × 6½in):

50cm × 25cm (20in × 10in) of cream Aida fabric, with 18 threads to 2.5cm (1in)
46cm × 20.5cm (18in × 8in) of cream lining fabric
40.5cm × 16cm (16in × 6¼in) of iron-on interfacing
Stranded embroidery cotton in the colours given in the panel
No26 tapestry needle
Pair of wooden hangers (for suppliers, see page 220)

●

THE EMBROIDERY

Prepare the fabric for your chosen design, marking the centre lines with basting stitches, and mount it in a frame (see page 9). In both cases, start to embroider from the centre of the design. For the cushion, use three strands of cotton in the needle for both the cross stitch and the backstitch.

The wall hanging is adapted from the cushion design, as seen in the picture. The stalk of the Timothy grass on the left-hand side is lowered so that it extends only over 32 threads from the upper leaf to the head: this is to balance the effect. Use two strands of thread in the needle for cross stitching and backstitching the grass stalks, and one thread for backstitching the finer details.

When you have finished your chosen design, gently steam press on the wrong side.

MAKING THE CUSHION COVER

With right sides together, and taking a 12mm (½in) seam, join the two pieces of strong cotton for the inner lining, leaving a 25cm (10in) opening at one side. Trim across the corners and turn the lining inside out. Insert the cushion pad and slip stitch the opening.

Trim the embroidered fabric to measure 48.5cm (19½in) square, keeping the design centred. Remove the central basting lines and, with right sides together, join the embroidered fabric and the cover backing fabric, again leaving a 25cm (10in) opening. Repeat the same process as for the inner lining.

To complete the cover, trim the edges with cord, forming it into loops at the corners and slip stitching it in place.

THE WALL HANGING

Centre the interfacing on the back of the embroidery and pin it in place. Remove the basting stitches and iron the interfacing in position. Trim the long edges of the embroidery until it measures 19cm (7½in) wide. Turn in the long edges by 12mm (½in) and press.

On the two short edges, make a 6mm (¼in) turning. Make a second turning, 4cm (1½in) deep, taking the fabric over a rod at the top and bottom. Baste and neatly hem in place.

Turn in the long edges of the lining fabric by 12mm (½in) and turn in the short edges so that the piece will neatly cover all raw edges and hems at the back of the work. Slip stitch in place.

FOXGLOVE CUSHION ▶		DMC	ANCHOR	MADEIRA
·	Cream	746	275	0101
I	Rose pink	3609	85	0710
∴	Medium rose	3608	86	0709
⊤	Deep rose	3607	87	0708
x	Dull pink	223	894	0812
⊥	Dusky pink	778	968	0808
⊔	Purplish red	315	896	0810
⊣	Lime green	472	264	1414
⊣	Bluish green	320	216	1311
	Pale green*	522	859	1513
—	Green	3348	264	1409
Υ	Medium green	3347	266	1408
+	Dark green	3346	817	1407
⊐	Very dark green	3345	268	1406
⊋	Light fawn	3047	886	2205
⊢	Fawn	612	832	2108

Note: bks foxglove bells in purplish red, Timothy grass stalks and leaf in bluish green and seeds in lime green, bent grass stalk in pale green, ground elder flower stalks in dark green, red campion stalks and flower in green, and style of dead foxglove flower in deep rose; for the wallhanger, you will not need dull pink, dusky pink, fawn, light fawn, pale green, very dark green, and green.*

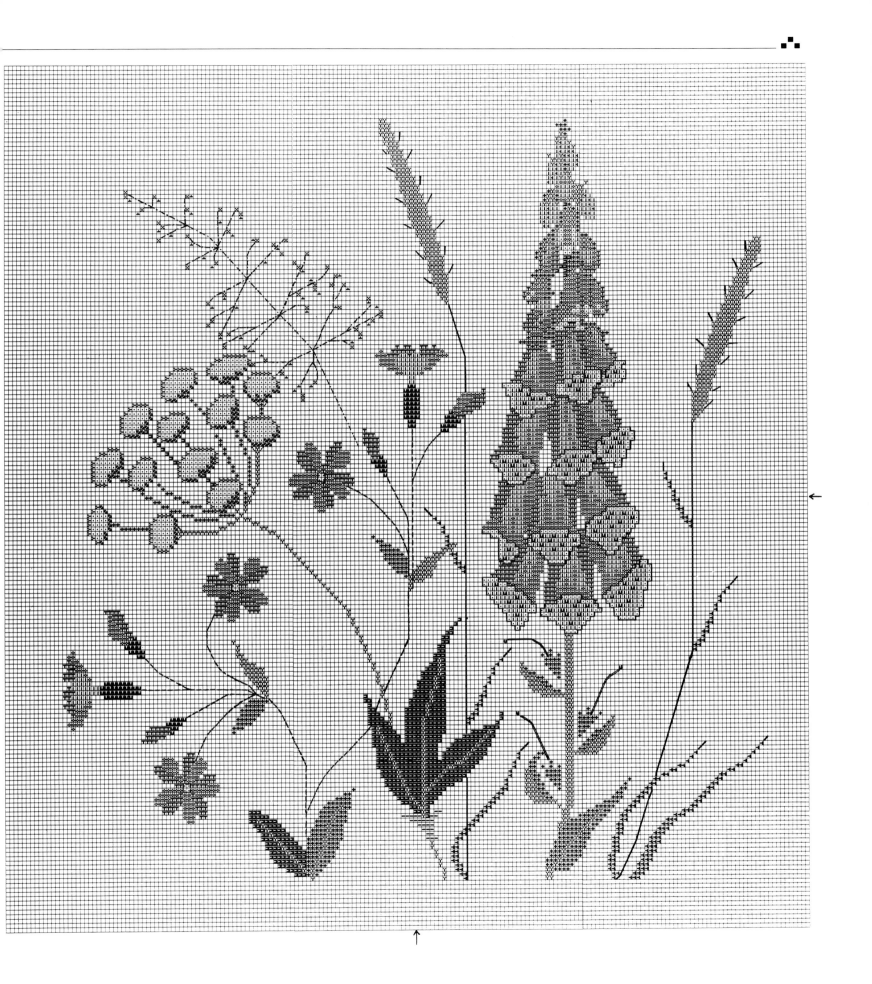

Floral Correspondence

Any keen gardener or flower-arranger would be happy to receive one of these cross-stitched greetings cards or a gift with a hand-embroidered tag, depicting a vibrant orange lily, or the more exotic passion flower.

FLORAL CORRESPONDENCE

YOU WILL NEED

For the Lily Card, measuring 20.5cm × 15cm (8in × 6in), with an oval portrait cut-out measuring 14cm × 9cm (5½in × 3½in):

19cm × 14cm (7½in × 5½in) of cream, 18-count Aida fabric
19cm × 14cm (7½in × 5½in) of iron-on interfacing
Stranded embroidery cotton in the colours given in the panel
No 26 tapestry needle
Greetings card, for suppliers see page 220

For the Passion Flower Card, measuring 20.5cm × 15cm (8in × 6in), with an oval portrait cut-out, measuring 14cm × 9cm (5½in × 3½in):

19cm × 14cm (7½in × 5½in) of eau-de-Nil, 18-count Aida fabric
19cm × 14cm (7½in × 5½in) of iron-on interfacing
Stranded embroidery cotton in the colours given in the panel
No 26 tapestry needle
Greetings card, for suppliers see page 220

For the *Lavatera* Stationery Compendium, measuring 21.5cm × 15cm (8½ × 6in), with an oval portrait cut-out measuring 16cm × 10cm (6½in × 4in):

20cm × 14cm (8in × 5½in) of cream, 18-count Aida fabric
20cm × 14cm (8in × 5½in) of iron-on interfacing
Stranded embroidery cotton in the colours given in the panel
No 26 tapestry needle
Stationery set, from good needlework shops

For each Gift Tag, with an overall measurement of 12cm × 5cm (5in × 2in), folded to give a front panel 5cm (2in) square, with a cut-out 4cm (1½in) in diameter:

6.5cm (2½in) square of cream, 22-count Hardanger
6.5cm (2½in) square of iron-on interfacing
Stranded embroidery cotton in the colours given in the panel
No 26 tapestry needle
Gift tag, for suppliers see page 220

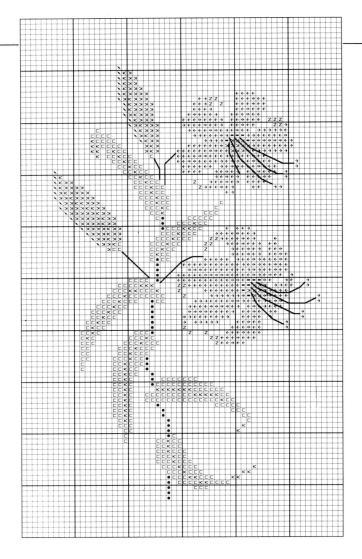

CARDS AND STATIONERY COMPENDIUM

The motifs for the two cards and the stationery compendium are stitched in the same way. Note that it is important to avoid excessive overstitching on the back, as this causes unsightly lumps to show on the right side. Prepare the fabric, marking the centre lines of each design with basting stitches. Complete the cross stitching, using two strands of cotton in the needle throughout. Steam press on the wrong side when complete.

Iron the interfacing to the back of the embroidery, and trim both to measure about 12mm (½in) larger all around than the cut-out window. Position the embroidery behind the window. Open out the self-adhesive mount and centre the embroidery behind the aperture.

Fold the card and press firmly to secure. Some cards may require a dab of glue to ensure a secure and neat finish.

GIFT TAGS

The designs for the lily, the passion flower and the *lavatera* gift tags are simply a single flower taken from each of the larger designs. For each, use one strand of thread in the needle for both cross stitch

LILY ◄		DMC	ANCHOR	MADEIRA
▬	Brown	898	360	2006
☒	Very deep yellow	741	304	0201
◥	Deep yellow	742	303	0107
→	Dark orange	900	333	0208
←	Orange	946	332	0207
⊞	Light orange	970	316	0204
●	Dark green	3051	846	1508
⊏	Green	3363	262	1602
K	Pale green	3364	260	1603
⊠	Yellow	743	297	0113

Note: bks stamens in brown, and stems in dark green.

and backstitch. Embroider from the centre. Steam press the embroidery on the wrong side.

Iron the interfacing to the back of the embroidery, and trim both to measure 6mm (¼in) larger all around than the cut-out window. This will prevent the mounted picture from wrinkling. Position the embroidery behind the window.

Open out the self-adhesive mount and centre the embroidery behind the aperture.

Fold the card and press firmly to secure. Some cards may require a dab of glue to ensure a secure and neat finish.

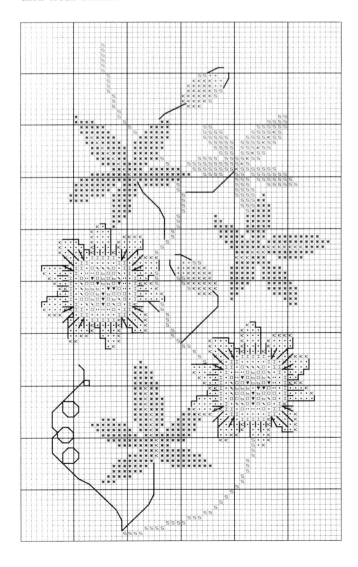

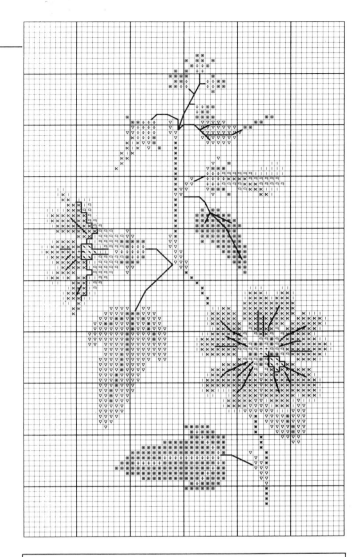

LAVATERA ▲		DMC	ANCHOR	MADEIRA
◥	Lemon	727	293	0110
✳	Dark green	3051	846	1508
▽	Mid green	3363	262	1602
⊙	Pale green	3053	859	1510
÷	Light grey green	644	830	1907
↑	Dark red	915	89	0705
⊟	Purplish pink	3607	87	0708
⊠	Pink	3608	86	0709
⊡	Pale pink	3609	85	0710

Note: bks around the centres of the flowers in brown (used for bks only), the stalk of the top bud in dark green, all other stalks and veins of top leaf in pale green, and the markings on the petals in dark red; the veins of the small leaf worked in pale green are stitched in light grey green.*

PASSION FLOWER ◄		DMC	ANCHOR	MADEIRA
●	Ecru	Ecru	926	Ecru
◥	Yellow	743	297	0113
▢	Navy	939	127	1009
▼	Purplish brown	315	896	0810
··	Reddish brown	221	897	0811
✳	Dark green	890	879	1314
S	Green	3363	262	1602
⊔	Yellowish green	471	266	1501
K	Pale green	368	240	1310
+	Light green	3364	260	1603
I	Purple	552	101	0713

Note: bks the tips of the buds in light green, all stems and tendrils in green, and the fringe around the centre of the flower in purple.

Pansies and Roses

This delightful placemat and napkin will certainly enhance any table setting, whether for a candlelit dinner or a summer party. You might vary the shades of the roses and pansies to match either your table setting, or perhaps the flowers from your own garden. If you want to change the design to make up an alternative set, you could quite easily adapt the motif to fit a corner instead of running down the side.

PANSIES AND ROSES

YOU WILL NEED

For one Placemat, measuring 33cm × 47cm (13in × 19in), and one napkin, measuring 40cm (16in) square:

Ready-prepared placemat and napkin (for suppliers, see page 220), 26 threads to 2.5cm (1in)
Stranded embroidery cotton in the colours given in the panel
No24 tapestry needle

NOTE If you prefer not to use ready-prepared table linen, buy fabric with the same thread count. Work the embroidery first; trim to the correct size (including fringe), and withdraw a thread 12mm (½in) in from each edge. Neatly overcast every alternate thread, and then remove all cross threads below the stitched line to complete the fringe.

PREPARING THE FABRIC

First mark the centre (horizontal) line along the length of the placemat with a line of basting stitches. Measure in 2.5cm (1in) from the start of the fringe on the right-hand side and make a vertical line of basting stitches. Position the centre of the motif on the horizontal line of basting stitches and the right-hand edge of the motif along the vertical line of basting stitches. For the napkin, measure in and baste lines 12mm (½in) in from the edge, at one corner, as base lines for positioning.

Stretch the placemat or napkin in a frame (see page 10).

THE EMBROIDERY

Start at the centre of the appropriate motif and, using two strands of embroidery cotton in the needle, work each stitch over two threads of fabric in each direction. Make sure that all the top crosses run in the same direction and that each row is worked into the same holes as the top or bottom of the preceding row, so that you do not leave a space between rows.

Gently steam press the finished work on the wrong side to remove all creases.

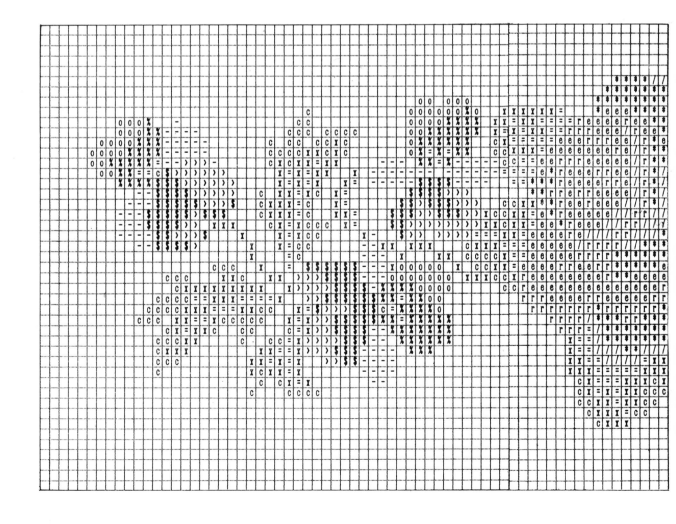

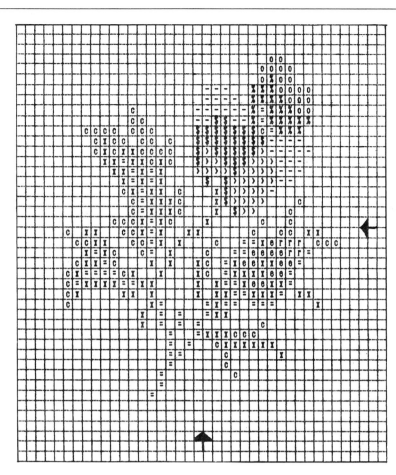

PANSIES AND ROSES		DMC	ANCHOR	MADEIRA
‡	Light pink	3609	85	0710
∕	Medium pink	3608	86	0709
r	Dark pink	718	88	0707
e	Darkest pink	915	89	0705
−	Light mauve	210	108	0803
⟩	Medium mauve	208	111	0804
$	Dark mauve	562	210	1202
%	Light yellow	3078	292	0102
o	Dark yellow	743	301	0113
c	Light green	3052	844	1509
x	Medium green	3347	266	1408
=	Dark green	3051	845	1508

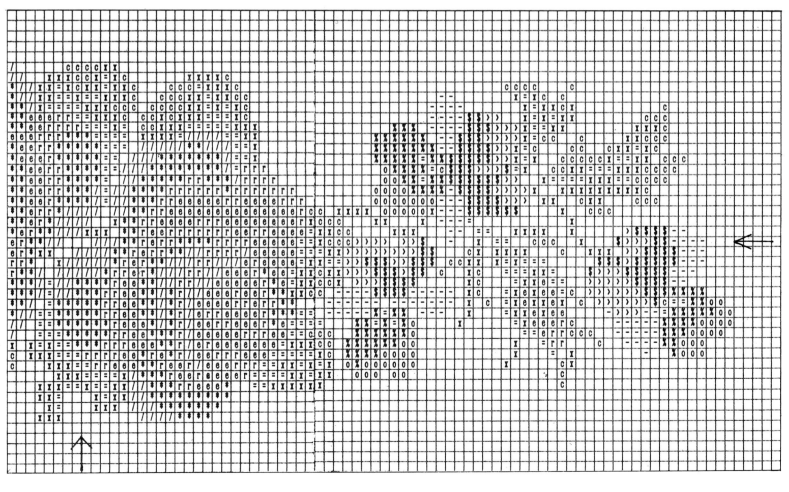

Poppy Picture and Frame

The bright red of fragile poppies growing among stems of bearded barley is used here to create a striking picture. To complete the effect, the same design has been used for an eye-catching surround for a favourite photograph.

POPPY PICTURE
AND FRAME

YOU WILL NEED

For the Poppy Picture, measuring 27cm × 22cm (10¾in × 8¾in) when framed:

33cm × 27.5cm (13in × 11in) of cream, 18-count Aida
Stranded embroidery cotton in the colours given in the panel
No26 tapestry needle
Strong thread, for lacing across the back when mounting
Cardboard for mounting
Frame of your choice

For the photograph frame, measuring 27cm × 22cm (10¾in × 8¾in), with an aperture measuring 14cm × 9cm (5½in × 3½in):

25.5cm × 20.5cm (10¼in × 8¼in) of white, 14-count perforated paper
Stranded embroidery cotton in the colours given in the panel
No24 tapestry needle
25.5cm × 20.5cm (10¼in × 8¼in) of iron-on interfacing
Frame of your choice

●

THE EMBROIDERY

For the picture, prepare the fabric and mark the horizontal and vertical centre lines with basting stitches in a light-coloured thread. Stretch the fabric in an embroidery frame, following the instructions on page 9. Begin at the centre and work out, using two strands of embroidery cotton in the needle for both cross stitch and backstitching. Gently steam press the finished embroidery.

For the frame, find the centre of the perforated paper by counting the spaces between holes. Mark this point with a soft pencil, and then count out to a convenient starting point on the border. Use three strands of embroidery cotton in the needle for both cross stitch and backstitching. When you have completed your design, cut out the central aperture. Mark the line first with a soft pencil and cut with a sharp craft knife.

MOUNTING AND FRAMING

For the picture, mark the central horizontal and vertical lines on the cardboard to be used for mounting and align these with the lines of basting stitches. Lace the embroidery over the mount, following the instructions on page 13, and remove basting stitches. Set the mount in a frame of your choice.

For the frame, iron the interfacing to the back of the embroidered perforated paper and then use a craft knife to trim the interfacing to the same size, including the aperture. Insert the embroidered paper into the frame of your choice.

POPPY PICTURE

POPPY FRAME

Note: one skein of each colour will complete both designs, but if you are only making the frame you will not require the dark brown; poppy picture bks the stamens of the seed heads in black, barley whiskers and soil in fawn, highlights on the seed pod in yellowish green, lines separating the barley grains in cream, soil in dark brown, and poppy bud stems in green; for the frame bks barley whiskers in fawn, lines separating barley grains in cream, tip of barley leaf in pale green, and poppy bud stems in green.

POPPIES		DMC	ANCHOR	MADEIRA
	Cream*	746	275	0101
↑	Red	349	13	0212
⊠	Deep red	498	19	0511
◪	Maroon	902	897	0601
⋈	Light orange	608	330	0206
☐	Orange red	606	335	0209
▬	Deep orange	900	333	0208
⊿	Deep salmon	3340	329	0301
⊠	Pale green	3053	859	1510
⊞	Green	3347	266	1408
◥	Medium green	3346	817	1407
▼	Dark green	3345	268	1406
⊟	Yellowish green	472	264	1414
◻	Fawn	372	887	2110
⊞	Dark brown	3031	905	2003
■	Black	310	403	Black

Photograph Album and Pillow

For that christening present with a difference, here is an easy-to-make cover for an album of treasured photographs. The cover is decorated with delicate, pastel-shaded sweet peas. To complement this, why not embroider a baby's pillow with matching flowers?

PHOTOGRAPH ALBUM AND PILLOW

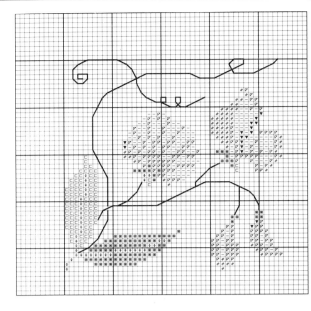

YOU WILL NEED

For the cover to fit a baby's Photograph Album, measuring 21.5cm × 16cm (8½in × 6¼in):

68cm × 19cm (27in × 7½in) of cream, 18-count Aida fabric
47cm × 16.5cm (18½in × 6½in) of white interfacing
Stranded embroidery cotton in the colours given in the panel
No 26 tapestry needle

For the baby's Pillow Cover, measuring 33cm (13in) square, including the broderie anglaise edging:

12.5cm (5in) square of white, 18-count Aida fabric, for the embroidered motif
32cm (12½in) square of white damask, for the front of the pillow
28cm × 32cm (11in × 12½in) and another strip 10cm × 32cm (4in × 12½in), both of white damask, for the back of the pillow
1.8m (1¾yds) of frilled insertion broderie anglaise, 5cm (2in) wide
1.8m (1¾yds) of pink or blue ribbon, of an appropriate width to slot through your broderie anglaise
Stranded embroidery cotton in the colours given in the panel
No 26 tapestry needle

•

THE ALBUM COVER

Fold the Aida in half, giving you a working area 34cm × 19cm (13½in × 7½in). With the fold on the left, measure in 19mm (¾in) from the fold and baste from top to bottom. From this line, measure a further 21.5cm (8½in) across and baste another line from top to bottom. From the top edge, measure down 15mm (⅔in) and from the bottom edge measure up 15mm (⅔in). Baste along these two lines. This will leave you with a rectangular area 21.5cm × 16cm (8½in × 6¼in) for the front cover of your album.

Position your embroidery either centrally within this area or slightly towards the bottom left-hand corner, whichever you prefer. Use two strands of cotton for the cross stitch, two strands for back-

stitching the stalks and tendrils, and one strand for backstitching the fine detail on the seed pods.

Gently steam press on the wrong side when complete.

MAKING UP THE COVER

Centre the interfacing lengthwise on the Aida fabric. Fold the Aida to form a narrow hem along all the edges, enclosing the interfacing, and machine stitch in position. Centre the album on the wrong side of the fabric and fold the extra width over the front and over the back cover. Seam along the edges at the top and bottom to form a pocket at the front and back.

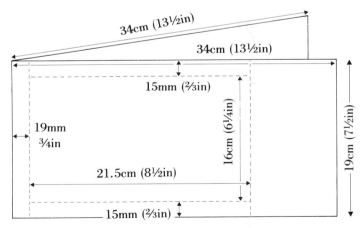

BABY'S PILLOW COVER

Find the centre point of your square of Aida and, beginning from the centre of the pattern, embroider the sweet pea motif, using two strands of cotton in the needle, both for the cross stitch and for the backstitch. The sample has been worked in pink, but alternative shades of blue are given in the key to the motif design. Gently steam press on the wrong side when complete.

SWEET PEA PILLOW ◀		DMC	ANCHOR	MADEIRA
▼	Maroon	902	72	0601
▨	Deep pink	602	63	0702
▷	Pink	603	62	0701
−	Pale pink	605	60	0613
⊏	Dark green	3345	268	1406
▣	Green	3346	817	1407
÷	Light green	3347	266	1408
Alternative blue shaded for boy				
▼	Dark blue	333	119	0903
▨	Blue	340	118	0902
▷	Light mauve	210	108	0802
−	Pale mauve	211	342	0801
⊏	Dark green	3345	268	1406
▣	Green	3346	817	1407
÷	Light green	3347	266	1408

Note: whether the pillow is for a boy or girl, bks flower stalk in green and tendrils in dark green.

SWEET PEA ALBUM COVER ▼		DMC	ANCHOR	MADEIRA
▼	Black	310	403	Black
▶	Dark blue	333	119	0903
▢	Navy	939	127	1009
◇	Blue	340	118	0902
◩	Pale blue	341	117	0901
▼	Maroon	902	72	0601
▨	Deep pink	602	63	0702
▷	Pink	603	62	0701
−	Pale pink	605	60	0613
✳	Dark green	3345	268	1406
⑤	Medium green	3346	817	1407
ⓑ	Green	3347	266	1408
Ⓚ	Yellowish green	472	264	1414
⌐	Purple	208	110	0804
Ⅰ	Mauve	209	109	0803
△	Light mauve	210	108	0802
⊓	Pale mauve	211	342	0801
↑	Reddish purple	550	102	0714

Note: bks all branches and tendrils in medium green, and the calyx of the pea pods in dark green.

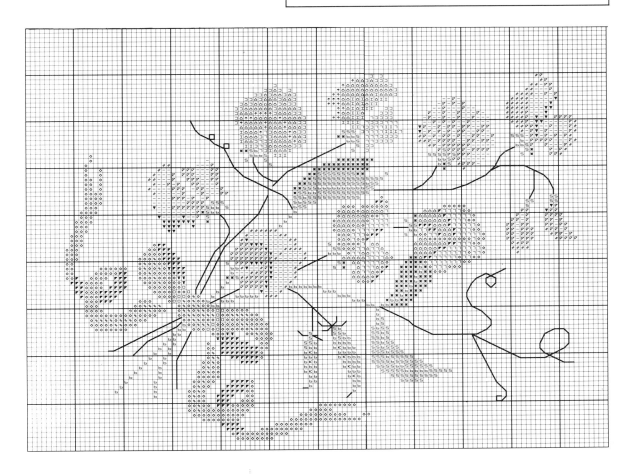

MAKING UP THE PILLOW

Make a narrow hem on one of the 32cm (12½in) sides of the larger back piece of the damask, and repeat on one of the 32cm (12½in) sides of the narrow strip.

Cut a 9cm (3½in) square from the top left corner of the front piece of damask, and snip the inner corner of the cut area to facilitate the turning of a 6mm (¼in) hem along the two cut sides. Insert the embroidered motif and machine along the two sides.

With all right sides together, place the back piece of damask on the larger front piece and then the narrower strip, overlapping the two. Machine around all four sides. Turn right side out and press.

Machine the broderie anglaise into place all around the pillow on the extreme edge, mitring the corners. Slip a ready-made cot or pram pillow into the finished cover.

113

Small Gifts

A peach rose on the pincushion is edged with a delicate cream border, echoed by broderie anglaise. The bag, filled with lavender from your garden, will remind you of summer throughout the rest of the year. To complete the trio, there is a bookmark with a lacy trim.

SMALL GIFTS

YOU WILL NEED

For the Pincushion, measuring 17.5cm (7in) square, excluding the lace:

25cm (10in) square of cream, 14-count Aida fabric
20cm (8in) square of cream backing fabric
1.6m (1¾yds) of cream broderie anglaise, 5cm (2in) wide
4 pale peach ribbon roses
Stranded embroidery cotton in the colours given in the panel
No24 tapestry needle
Polyester filling

For the Lavender Bag, measuring 12.5cm × 17cm (5in × 6¾in):

20cm x 22cm (8in x 8½in) of cream 14-count Aida fabric
15cm × 17cm (6in × 6½in) of cream backing fabric
35cm (14in) of cream broderie anglaise, 5cm (2in) wide
50cm (20in) of peach satin ribbon, 6mm (¼in) wide
Stranded embroidery cotton in the colours given in the panel
No24 tapestry needle

For the Bookmark, measuring 9cm × 20.5cm (3½in × 8in):

Stranded embroidery cotton in the colours given in the panel
No24 tapestry needle
Prepared bookmark, in ivory (for suppliers, see page 220)

•

THE EMBROIDERY

Stretch the fabric for the pincushion or the lavender bag in a hoop or frame, as explained on page 9. The bookmark may be held in the hand when working the embroidery.

Following the correct chart, start the embroidery at the centre of the design, using two strands of embroidery cotton in the needle for the pincushion or lavender bag and one strand for the bookmark. Work each stitch over one block of fabric in each

direction. Make sure that all the top crosses run in the same direction and that each row is worked into the same holes as the top or bottom of the row before, so that you do not leave a space between rows. Lightly steam press the finished embroidery.

MAKING THE PINCUSHION

Trim the embroidery to measure 20cm (8in) square. Using a tiny french seam, join the short edges of the broderie anglaise together, then run a gathering thread close to the straight edge of the lace. Pulling up the gathers to fit, lay the lace on the right side of the embroidery, with the decorative edge facing inward and the straight edge parallel to the edge of the fabric and just inside the 12mm (½in) seam allowance. Baste in position, adjusting the gathers to allow extra fullness at the corners. Machine in place.

With right sides together, pin and machine the backing fabric and the embroidered piece together, enclosing the broderie anglaise edging and leaving a gap of 5cm (2in) at one side. Trim across the corners; turn the pincushion right side out, and insert the polyester filling. Slip stitch the opening to close it.

Lavender bag ▼

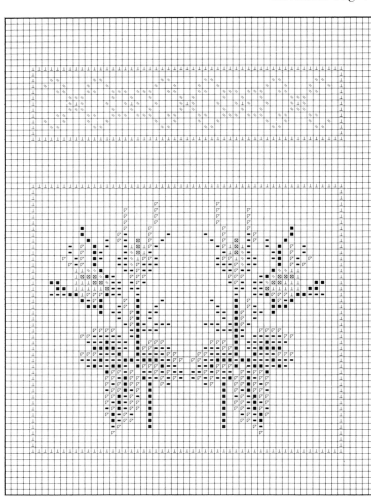

MAKING THE LAVENDER BAG

Trim the embroidered fabric to measure 15cm × 17cm (6in × 6½in). With right sides together, baste and machine stitch the embroidery to the backing fabric, stitching down the sides and across the bottom and taking a 12mm (½in) seam allowance.

Turn to the right side. Turn a single 12mm (½in) hem around the top. Join the short edges of the broderie anglaise with a tiny french seam, then run a gathering thread close to the straight edge of the lace. Pulling up the gathers to fit and with the right side of the lace to the wrong side of the bag, baste and then machine stitch the broderie anglaise in place around the top of the bag. Gently steam press.

Fill the bag with lavender and tie with a ribbon, placing it around the space between the two areas of embroidery.

BOOKMARK, LAVENDER BAG AND PINCUSHION ▼		DMC	ANCHOR	MADEIRA
◻	Cream	746	275	0101
⊥	Light peach	353	6	0304
⊠	Dark peach	352	9	0303
◹	Light green	3348	264	1409
▪	Medium green	3052	844	1509
◼	Dark green*	936	263	1507

Dark green used for bks outline of roses on pincushion only.

Bookmark ▼

Pincushion ▼

Traditional Sampler

This sampler would have looked perfectly at home hanging in a Victorian parlour around the turn of the century. A selection of traditional motifs of flowers and birds have been arranged to make this attractive design. Three of the motifs have been embroidered separately to make a delightful trio of pictures, or perhaps you would like to create a bell pull from the motifs, giving a truly Victorian flavour to your decor.

TRADITIONAL SAMPLER

YOU WILL NEED

For the Sampler and each of the small pictures derived from it, you will need the following, plus the individual requirements specified below:

Stranded embroidery cotton in the colours given in the appropriate panel
No24 tapestry needle
Strong thread, for lacing across the back
Cardboard, for mounting, sufficient to fit into the frame recess
Frame of your choice

For the Sampler, with a design area measuring 34cm × 25.5cm (13½in × 10¼in), or 183 stitches by 138 stitches, here in a frame measuring 40cm × 32.5cm (16in × 13in):

44cm × 35cm (17½in × 14in) of cream fabric, with 27 threads to 2.5cm (1in)

For the Rose picture, with a design area measuring 12cm × 13cm (4½in × 5in), or 64 stitches by 70 stitches, here in a frame measuring 18.5cm (7½in) square:

22cm × 23cm (8½in × 9in) of cream fabric, with 27 threads to 2.5cm (1in)

For the Cornflower picture, with a design area measuring 15cm × 11cm (6in × 4¼in), or 83 stitches by 59 stitches, here in a frame measuring 21cm × 16.5cm (8¼in × 6½in):

25cm × 21cm (10in × 8¼in) of cream fabric, with 27 threads to 2.5cm (1in)

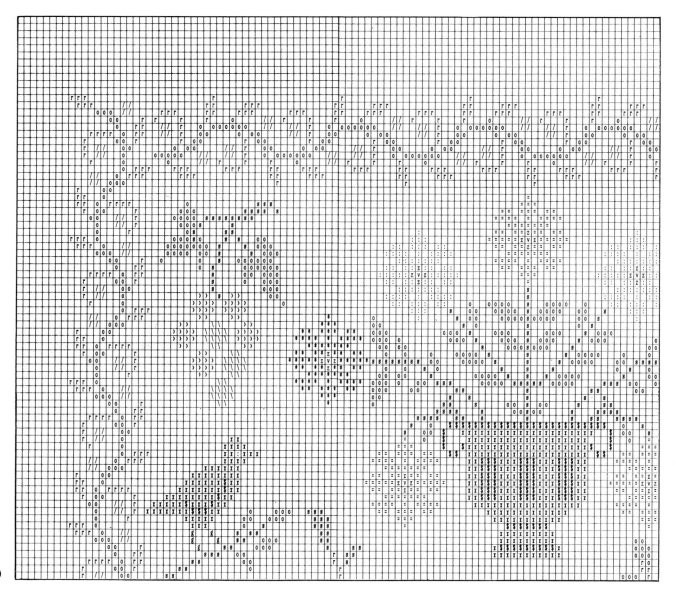

CHART 1

For the Bird picture, with a design area measuring 11cm × 8cm (4¼n × 3in), or 59 stitches by 44 stitches, here in a frame measuring 16.5cm × 13.5cm (6½in × 5¼in):

21cm × 18cm (8¼in × 7¼in) of cream fabric, with 27 threads to 2.5cm (1in)

•

THE EMBROIDERY

For each design, prepare the linen and stretch in a frame as explained on page 9. Following the chart, start the embroidery at the centre of the design, using two strands of embroidery cotton in the needle. Embroider each stitch over two threads of fabric in each direction. Make sure that all the top crosses run in the same direction and each row is worked into the same holes as the row before so

that you do not leave a space between the rows. Work the butterfly feelers with two strands of dark brown cotton in backstitch.

MAKING UP

Gently steam press the work on the wrong side and mount it as explained on page 13. To retain the traditional feel of the sampler, choose a simple wooden frame without a cardboard mount.

NOTE
The sampler has been divided into four charts, each showing a quarter.
The key and Charts 3 and 4 are on pages 124-5.

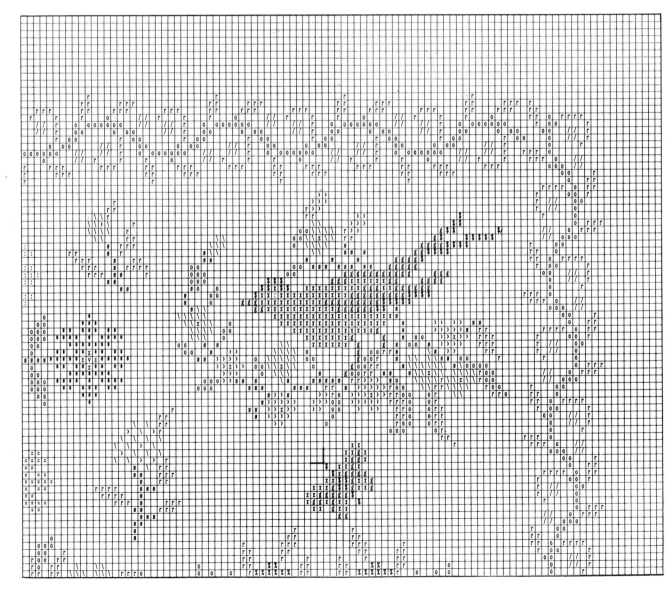

CHART 2

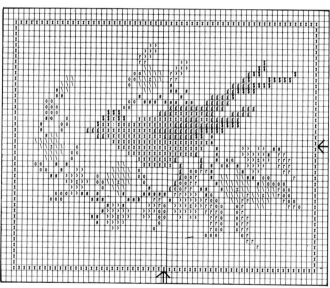

BIRD ▲		DMC	ANCHOR	MADEIRA
╲	Light mauve	341	117	0901
⟨	Dark mauve	340	118	0902
g	Gold	834	874	2204
z	Dark yellow	725	298	0113
‡	Light blue	3325	976	1002
o	Light green	471	265	1502
r	Medium green	988	244	1402
s	Dark green	986	246	1404
x	Light brown	612	832	2002
s	Dark brown	370	856	2201

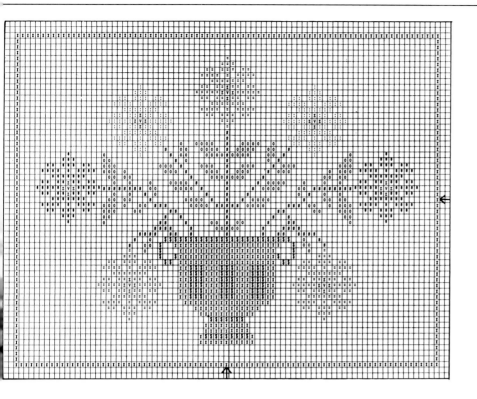

CORNFLOWER ◄		DMC	ANCHOR	MADEIRA
v	Light yellow	727	293	0110
z	Dark yellow	725	306	0108
‡	Light blue	3325	976	1002
:	Medium blue	334	977	1003
=	Dark blue	312	979	1005
o	Light green	471	265	1502
s	Dark green	986	246	1404
x	Light brown	612	832	2002
$	Dark brown	370	856	2201

ROSE ▼		DMC	ANCHOR	MADEIRA
%	Pale magenta	3609	85	0710
v	Light yellow	727	295	0111
z	Dark yellow	725	298	0113
o	Light green	471	265	1502
r	Medium green	988	244	1402
s	Dark green	986	246	1404
x	Light brown	612	832	2002
$	Dark brown	370	856	2201

TRADITIONAL SAMPLER		DMC	ANCHOR	MADEIRA
/	Light pink	224	894	0813
<	Dark pink	3721	896	0811
\	Light mauve	341	117	0901
>	Dark mauve	340	118	0902
%	Pale magenta	3609	85	0710
v	Light yellow	727	295	0111
z	Dark yellow	725	298	0113
g	Gold	834	874	2204
‡	Light blue	3325	379	1912
:	Medium blue	334	977	1003
=	Dark blue	312	979	1005
o	Light green	471	265	1502
r	Medium green	988	244	1402
s	Dark green	986	246	1404
x	Light brown	612	832	2002
$	Dark brown	370	856	2201

124

CHART 3

CHART 1	CHART 2
CHART 3	CHART 4

CHART 4

ROMANTIC MOMENTS

A wedding is a great family occasion so why not add your congratulations in cross stitch with a beautiful wedding sampler? Alternatively, you could choose something that is quicker to stitch, such as a picture, greetings card or gift tag for the happy couple.

WEDDING BELLS

YOU WILL NEED

For the Wedding Bells sampler, with a design area measuring 24cm × 25cm (9½in × 10in), or 124 stitches by 129 stitches, here in a frame measuring 36cm × 38cm (14½in × 15¼in):

34cm × 35cm (13½in × 14in) of white evenweave fabric, with 25 threads to 2.5cm (1in)
Stranded embroidery cotton in the colours given in the panel
No24 tapestry needle
Strong thread, for lacing across the back
Cardboard for mounting, sufficient to fit into the frame recess
Frame of your choice

•

THE EMBROIDERY

Prepare the fabric and stretch it in a frame as explained on page 9. Following the chart, start the embroidery at the centre of the design, using two strands of embroidery cotton in the needle. Work each stitch over two threads of fabric in each direction. Make sure that all the top crosses run in the same direction and that each row is worked into the same holes as the top or bottom of the row before, so that you do not leave a space between the rows.

With backstitch and using one strand of dark grey cotton, outline the bells and flowers, then embroider the date, month and year with two strands of dark grey cotton. The flower stalks are worked with two strands of medium green cotton in backstitch.

Work the centres of the blue flowers with french knots in light peach cotton.

MAKING UP

Gently steam press the work on the wrong side and mount it as explained on page 13. Choose an appropriate frame and mount to add the final touch to this record of a very special day.

WEDDING BELLS ▼		DMC	ANCHOR	MADEIRA
⊡	Light pink	3689	66	0606
H	Dark pink	3688	68	0605
⊟	Light mauve	211	108	0801
⊓	Light green	3348	264	1409
⊞	Light peach	353	9	0304
◹	Dark peach	758	9575	0403
‖	Light blue	800	128	0908
╱	Medium blue	799	130	0910
S	Dark blue	798	131	0911
⋈	Dark mauve	210	109	0803
X	Medium green	3052	844	1509
▲	Dark green	936	263	1507
◇	Light grey	415	398	1803
■	Dark grey	414	399	1801

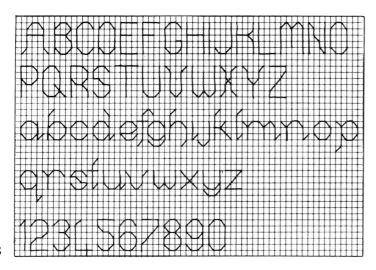

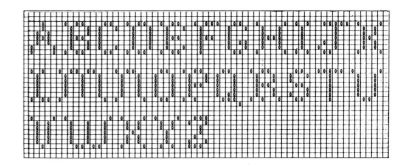

A Special Day

Bluebirds, hearts, roses and ribbons in soft shades of peach and delicate blue – these are the perfect accessories for a wedding. These motifs have been used in various ways to create a range of pretty and lasting gifts and mementoes for the bridal couple or other members of the wedding group.

A SPECIAL DAY

YOU WILL NEED

For the Coaster, measuring 5.5cm (2¼in) in diameter:

12.5cm (5in) square of antique white, 18-count Aida fabric
Stranded embroidery cotton in the colours given in the appropriate panel
No26 tapestry needle
Glass coaster, for suppliers see page 220

For the Card, with a rectangular aperture measuring 13cm × 7cm (5¼in × 3¾in):

12.5cm × 18cm (5in × 7½in) of antique white, 18-count Aida fabric
Peach-coloured ribbon trim, 7mm (⅓in) wide, if desired
Stranded embroidery cotton in the colours given in the appropriate panel
No26 tapestry needle
Card, for suppliers see page 220

For the Picture, set in an oval frame measuring 7cm × 5.5cm (2⅞in × 2¼in):

15cm × 20cm (6in × 8in) of antique white, 18-count Aida fabric
Stranded embroidery cotton in the colours given in the appropriate panel
No26 tapestry needle
Silver frame, for suppliers see page 220

For the Placecard:

Small remnant piece of antique white, 18-count Aida fabric
Stranded embroidery cotton in the colours given in the appropriate panel
No26 tapestry needle
Placecard, for suppliers see page 220

For the Gift Card:

Small remnant piece of antique white, 18-count Aida linen
Peach ribbon, 3mm (⅛in) wide, for a trim
Stranded embroidery cotton in the colours given in the appropriate panel
No26 tapestry needle
Gift card, for suppliers see page 220

NOTE: *You will also require some graph paper and a pencil, to work out the names and dates. The panel lists all the colours used in the complete range of projects, so check which colours are used in your chosen project(s) and buy one skein each of those particular colours only.*

•

PLANNING THE DESIGN

Several alphabets and numerals have been provided with these designs, so that you can personalize the items by adding names for initials and dates. Work these out on graph paper (each square represents one Aida block). Ensure that names and dates are centred under the other parts of the design, to give a pleasing effect. If the names are very long, you may need either to use a smaller alphabet or to stitch the initials only.

Each design uses only a small amount of fabric, which makes these projects an ideal way of using up off-cuts. On the other hand, if you have no odd pieces of fabric, you may prefer to embroider designs in batches, to avoid waste.

For each design, prepare the fabric as described on page 9, and mark the horizontal and vertical centre lines with basting stitches in a light-coloured thread. Set the fabric in a hoop and count out from the centre to start stitching at a point convenient to you. Each design is stitched with one strand of thread throughout, to give a delicate effect.

Work all cross stitches first, making sure that all top stitches run in the same direction. Finally, work all backstitch details.

Gently handwash the finished piece, if necessary, and lightly press with a steam iron on the wrong side. Follow the manufacturer's instructions for assembly.

A SPECIAL DAY ▶	DMC	ANCHOR	MADEIRA
• White	White	2	White
X Pale peach	754	1012	0305
P Medium peach	3779	868	0403
● Dark peach	758	9575	0402
S Medium grey green	522	860	1513

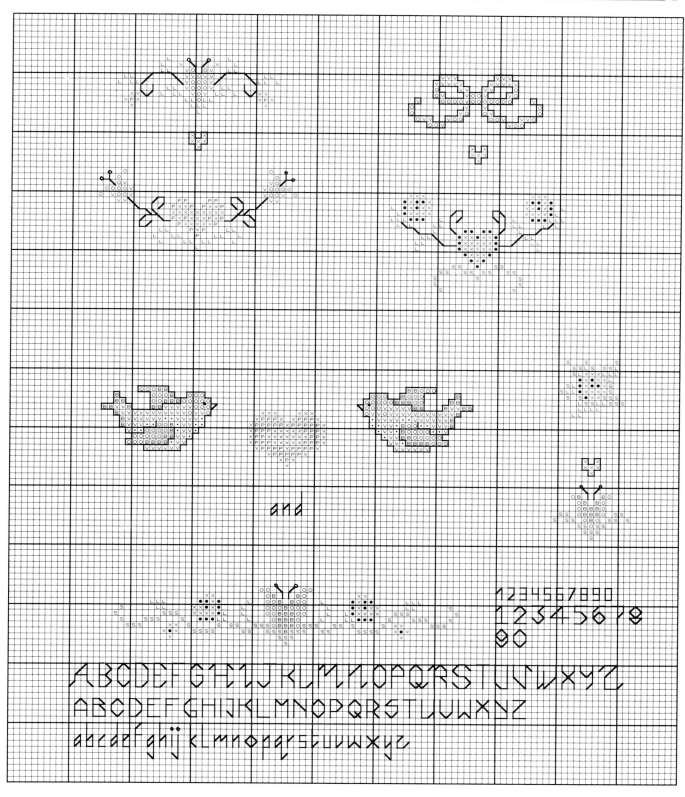

		DMC	ANCHOR	MADEIRA
L	Very light grey green	524	858	1511
V	Very light grey blue	928	900	1709
O	Light grey blue	927	849	1708
B	Medium grey blue	926	850	1707
	Medium steel grey*	646	815	1811

Note: for the coaster, backstitch the stems in medium grey green; the heart in dark peach, and lettering and stamens in medium steel grey*. For the card, make french knots for the eyes and backstitch the birds' outlines and beaks, and the lettering and stamens in medium steel grey*. For the oval picture, backstitch the bow outline in medium grey blue; the stems in medium grey green, and the heart in dark peach. For the gift card, backstitch the initials and heart in dark peach and the stamens in medium steel grey*. Medium steel grey* is used for backstitch only.

Romantic Alphabet

This lovely alphabet would be ideal
for enhancing wedding gifts.
A card and bookmark might include
the initials of both the bride and
groom, while guests' initials might
decorate placecards.

ROMANTIC ALPHABET

YOU WILL NEED

For the Card, measuring 9cm × 12cm
(3½in × 4¾in), with an aperture measuring
5.5cm × 7cm (2¼in × 2¾in):

*10cm (4in) square of 26-count, white evenweave
fabric*
*Stranded embroidery cotton in the colours given in
the panel*
No26 tapestry needle
Card, for suppliers see page 220)

For the Gift Tag, measuring 7cm × 5cm
(2¾in × 2in), with an aperture measuring
4cm (1½in) in diameter:

10cm (4in) square of 18-count, white Aida fabric
*Stranded embroidery cotton in the colours given
in the panel*
No26 tapestry needle
Gift tag, for suppliers see page 220

For the Bookmark, measuring 9cm × 20.5cm
(3½in × 8¼in), including the lace edging:

*Stranded embroidery cotton in the colours given
in the panel*
No26 tapestry needle
18-count Aida bookmark, for suppliers see page 220

For the Initial in an oval frame, measuring
5.5cm × 7cm (2¼in × 2¾in), with an aperture
measuring 4.5cm × 6cm (1¾in × 2⅜in):

*10cm × 15cm (4in × 6in) of 14-count, cream
Aida fabric*
*Stranded embroidery cotton in the colours given
in the panel*
No24 tapestry needle
Oval frame, for suppliers see page 220

For the Miniature Framed Initial, measuring
6.5cm (2½in) in diameter, with an aperture
measuring 5cm (2in) in diameter:

8cm (3¼in) square of 18-count, cream Aida fabric
*Stranded embroidery cotton in the colours given
in the panel*
No26 tapestry needle
Miniature metal frame, for suppliers see page 220

For the Napkin, measuring 40cm (16in) square:

*Stranded embroidery cotton in the colours given
in the panel*
No24 tapestry needle
*Ready-prepared ivory napkin, for suppliers see
page 220*

●

CARD

Prepare the fabric and mark the centre with horizontal and vertical lines of basting stitches. Mount it in a hoop as explained on page 9. Start the stitching at the centre, using two strands of cotton in the needle. Work each stitch over two fabric threads in each direction. Make sure that all the top crosses run in the same direction and that each row is worked into the same holes as the top and bottom of the row before, so that you do not leave a space between the rows.

MAKING UP

Gently steam press the embroidery on the wrong side and trim to within 12mm (½in) larger than the aperture. Centre your embroidery behind the opening and secure in place with double-sided tape.
Press the card firmly together.

GIFT TAG

This is made in the same way as the card, but you will have to use 18-count fabric for the embroidery.

BOOKMARK

Mark the centre of the bookmark from top to bottom with a line of basting stitches. Measure 4cm (1½in) up from the bottom of the bookmark and make another line of basting stitches. This will show you where to place the centre of your letter.
Start the stitching at the centre, using one strand of cotton in the needle. Work each stitch over one block of fabric in each direction. Make sure that all the top crosses run in the same direction, and that each row is worked into the same holes as the top or bottom of the row before, so that you do not leave a space between the rows. Gently steam press the finished embroidery on the wrong side.

INITIAL IN AN OVAL FRAME

Prepare the fabric and mark the centre with horizontal and vertical lines of basting stitches. Mount it in a hoop as explained on page 9.

Start the stitching at the centre, using two strands of cotton in the needle. Work each stitch over one block of fabric in each direction. Make sure that all the top crosses run in the same direction and that each row is worked into the same holes as the top or bottom of the row before, so that you do not leave a space between the rows.

MAKING UP

Gently steam press the embroidery on the wrong side. Using the white plastic back of the frame as a guide, place the embroidery centrally over the back and trim around the edge. Place the acetate front and embroidery face down in the frame and secure by clicking the back in place.

MINIATURE FRAMED INITIAL

Prepare the fabric and mark the centre with horizontal and vertical lines of basting stitches. Mount it in a hoop as explained on page 9. Start the stitching at the centre, using one strand of cotton in the needle. Work each stitch over one block of fabric in each direction. Make sure that all the top crosses run in the same direction and that each row is worked into the same holes as the top or bottom of the row before, so that you do not leave a space between the rows.

MAKING UP

Gently steam press the embroidery on the wrong side. Using the cream backing paper from the frame as a guide, place the embroidery centrally on the top and trim around the edge. Place the acetate, embroidery and cardboard disc face down in the frame and secure with the felt adhesive disc.

NAPKIN

Measure 4cm (1½in) vertically up from the bottom right hand corner and 4cm (1½in) horizontally in from the right-hand side and sew horizontal and vertical lines of basting stitches. The point at which they cross is the centre of the letter. Mount the napkin in a hoop as explained on page 9. Start the stitching at the centre of the chosen initial, using two strands of cotton in the needle. Work each stitch over two threads of fabric in each direction. Make sure that all the top crosses run in the same direction and that each row is worked into the same holes as the top or bottom of the row before, so that you do not leave a space between the rows. Gently steam press the embroidery on the wrong side.

ROMANTIC ALPHABET		DMC	ANCHOR	MADEIRA
X	Yellow	3078	292	0102
–	Light pink	3689	66	0606
<	Dark pink	3688	68	0605
=	Green	471	265	1502
Z	Grey	415	398	1803
	Dark green*	3345	268	1406

Note: bks outline using one strand of dark green* (used for bks only).

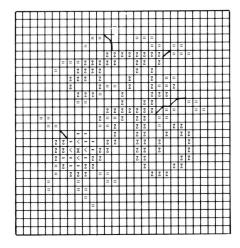

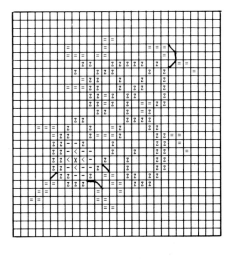

Turn to page 140 for charts for the remaining letters.

137

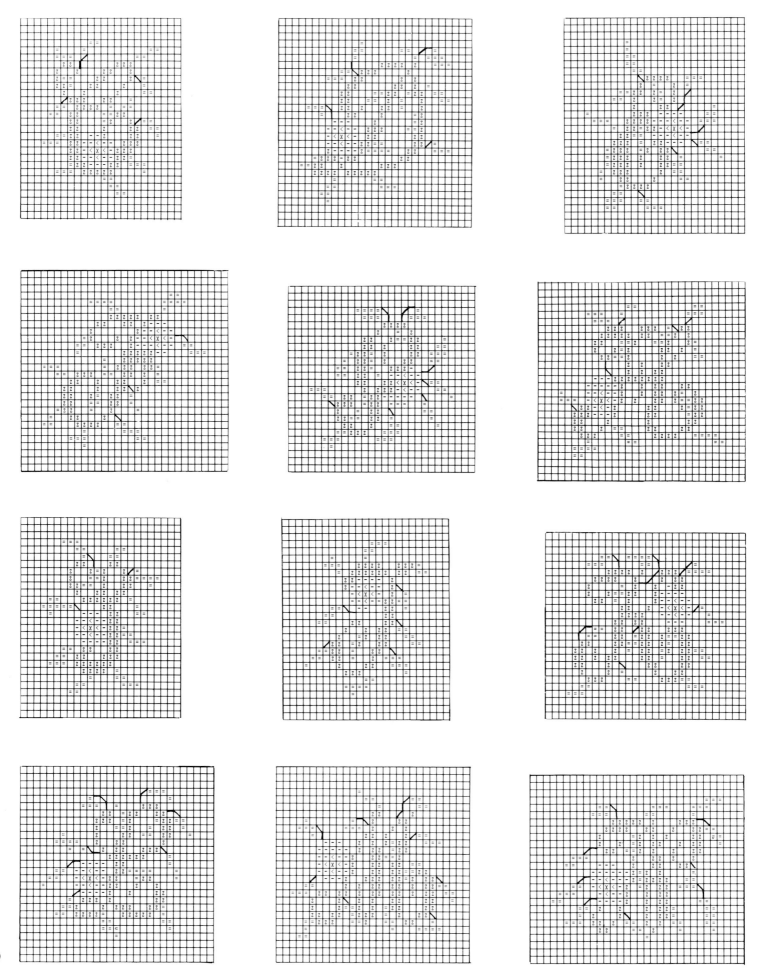

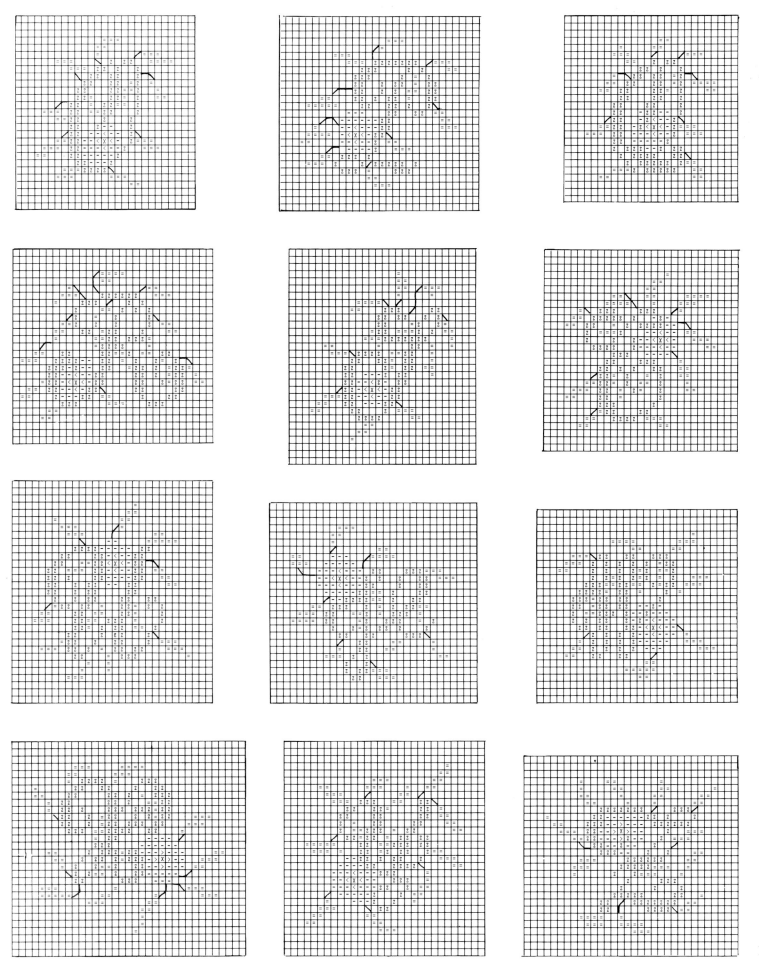

ANIMAL FRIENDS

Animals make a great subject for cross stitch designs, as can be seen in this chapter. You will see playful cats entangled in knitting wool, birds and butterflies decorating a sampler, and whales and dinosaurs wrapped around the initials of an alphabet.

KNITTING BAG

For each Knitting Bag, measuring
36.5cm × 32cm (14½in × 12½in):

*42cm × 76cm (16½in × 30in) of cream,
14-count Aida fabric
42cm × 76cm (16½in × 30in) of thin
polyester wadding
42cm × 76cm (16½in × 30in) of calico,
for the lining
Stranded embroidery cotton in the colours given in
the appropriate panels
No26 tapestry needle
Sewing thread to match the fabric
A pair of handles (for suppliers, see page 220)*

•

THE EMBROIDERY

Fold the embroidery fabric in half; press and
unfold. Taking the top (bag front) section, mark the
centre lines with basting stitches (see page 9) and
set it in a frame. Complete the cross stitching,
using two strands of thread in the needle, and then
the backstitching, using one strand. Ensure that
there is approximately 9cm (3½in) clearance at each
side of the finished embroidery (front section), 2.5cm
(1in) at the bottom, and 12.5cm (5in) at
the top.

Gently steam press the embroidered fabric on the
wrong side.

MAKING THE BAG

Pin, baste and stitch the batting to the wrong side
of the embroidered fabric, stitching around all sides
and taking a 1cm (½in) seam allowance. Trim the
batting back to the stitching line. Fold the fabric
in half, with right sides facing, and pin and baste
the side seams, taking a 1cm (½in) seam allowance
Stitch the side seams, stopping 16.5cm (6½in)
short of the top edge at each side.

Fold the lining in half, with right sides facing,
and stitch the side seams, as for the main fabric.
Turn the main fabric right side out and place the
lining inside the bag. Turn in the 12mm (½in)
allowance around the remaining raw edges and top
stitch them together, making sure that no lining is
visible on the right side. Thread the top edges of
the bag through the bag handles, gathering the
fabric evenly, and catch-stitch by hand to finish.

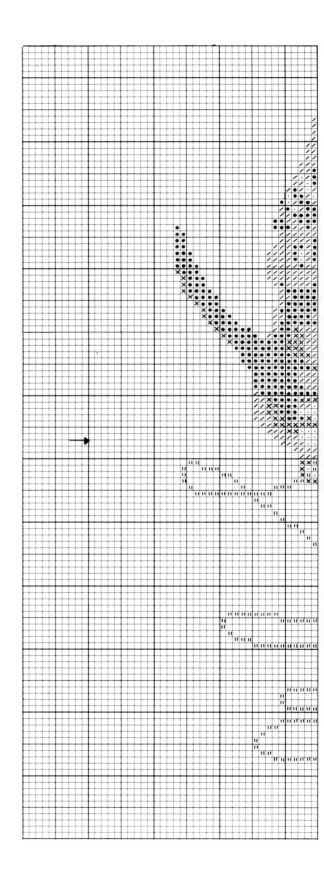

KNITTING BAG ▼	DMC	ANCHOR	MADEIRA
● Dark steel grey	413	401	1713
✕ Steel grey	414	400	1801
╱ Pale grey	415	398	1803
· White	White	2	White
‖ Medium pink	899	27	0505

Note: backstitch outline in pale grey.

Hedgerow Sampler

The traditional sampler is given a new look with this charming combination of blue tits, butterflies and berries. If you don't want to make a sampler, either the butterflies or the birds could be repeated to make a border, perhaps for a towel or a tablecloth.

HEDGEROW SAMPLER

YOU WILL NEED

For the Sampler, set in a frame with an aperture measuring 28.5cm × 24.5cm (11½in × 9½in):

*46cm × 38cm, (18in × 15in) of ivory,
11-count Aida fabric
Stranded embroidery cotton in the colours given
in the panel
No24 tapestry needle
Picture frame, with a cut-out as specified above
Firm card, to fit the frame
Lightweight synthetic wadding, the same
size as the card
Strong thread, for mounting
Glue stick
Four small black beads and a beading needle
(optional)*

•

THE EMBROIDERY

Prepare the fabric as described on page 9; find the centre either by folding the fabric in half and then in half again, and lightly pressing the folded corner, or by marking the horizontal and vertical centre lines with basting stitches in a light-coloured thread. Mount the fabric in a frame (see page 10) and start each design from the centre.

Following the chart, complete all the cross stitching first, using two strands of thread in the needle. Finish with the backstitching, again using two strands of thread. Be careful not to take dark threads across the back of the work in such a way that they show through on the right side.

The birds' eyes, indicated by black dots on the chart, can either be made with a single french knot for each, stitched with two strands of black thread, or you can use a small black bead for each eye.

MOUNTING AND FRAMING

Remove the embroidery from the frame and wash if necessary, then press lightly on the wrong side, using a steam iron and taking extra care if you have used beads for the eyes. Spread glue evenly on one side of the mounting card, and lightly press the wadding to the surface. Lace the embroidery over the padded surface (see page 13). Remove basting stitches, place the embroidery in the frame, and assemble the frame according to the manufacturer's instructions.

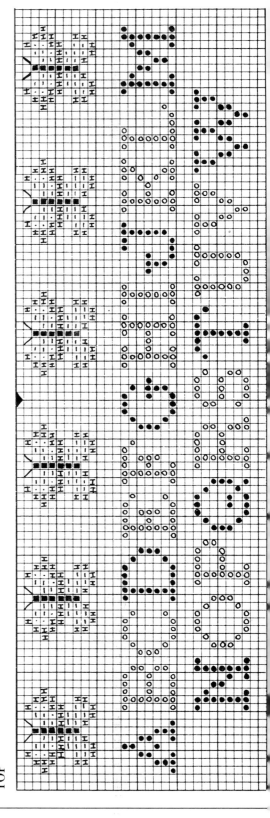

TOP

HEDGEROW SAMPLER ▲		ANCHOR	DMC	MADEIRA
H	Blue	979	312	1005
−	Light yellow green	278	472	1414
+	Medium yellow green	280	733	1609
V	Medium green	267	580	1608
∧	Dark green	268	935	1504

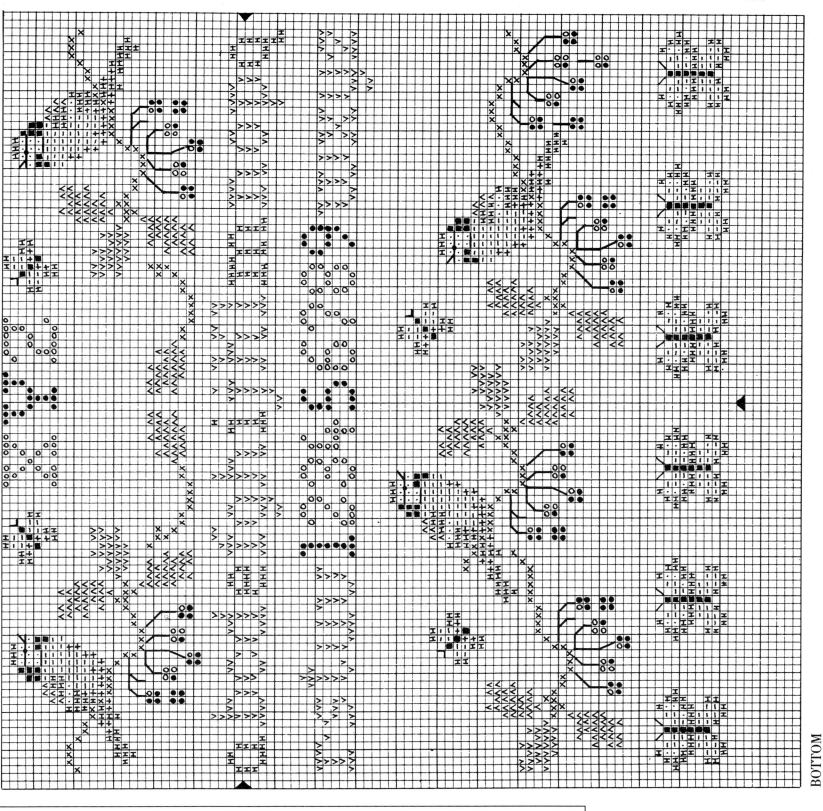

		ANCHOR	DMC	MADEIRA
·	White	1	Blanc	White
X	Brown	360	898	2006
■	Black	430	Black	Black
○	Bright red	19	817	212
●	Dark red	20	498	513

Note: bks the butterfly feelers, birds' eye lines and beaks in black, and the cherry stalks in dark green. Using two strands of thread in the needle, form each bird's eye with a french knot, unless using beads.

Lace-edged Cushions

These beautiful lace-edged cushions, with their amusing cartoon-style cats, are simple to make and will brighten up any child's room, either scattered on the bed, or on a favourite chair.

LACE-EDGED CUSHIONS

YOU WILL NEED

For each Cushion, measuring 20cm (8in) square,
excluding the lace edging:

*30cm (12in) square of white,
18-count Aida fabric
22.5cm (9in) of contrasting fabric to back
your cushion
2m (2¼yds) of white lace, 2.5cm (1in) deep
Stranded embroidery cotton in the colours given in
the panels
No26 tapestry needle
Sewing thread to match the fabric
A cushion pad, 21.5cm (8½in) square*

•

THE EMBROIDERY

Prepare the fabric, marking the centre lines of the
design with basting stitches, and mount it in a hoop
or frame, following the instructions on page 9.
Referring to the appropriate chart, complete the
cross stitching, starting at the centre and using two
strands in the needle throughout. Embroider the
main areas first, and then finish with the backstitching, this time using a single strand in the
needle. Steam press on the wrong side.

MAKING UP THE COVER

Trim the embroidery to measure 22.5cm (9in)
square. Using a tiny french seam, join the short
edges of the lace together. Run a gathering thread
close to the straight edge; pull up the gathers to fit
and, with the right side of the embroidery facing
and the lace lying on the fabric, baste the edging
to the outer edge, placing it just inside the 12mm
(½in) seam allowance. Adjust the gathers evenly,
allowing a little extra fullness at the corners.
Machine stitch the frill in place.

With right sides together, place the backing
fabric on top; baste and machine stitch around,
leaving a 15cm (6in) opening in the middle of one
side. Remove basting stitches; trim across the
corners, and turn the cover through. Insert the
cushion pad and slip stitch the opening to secure it.

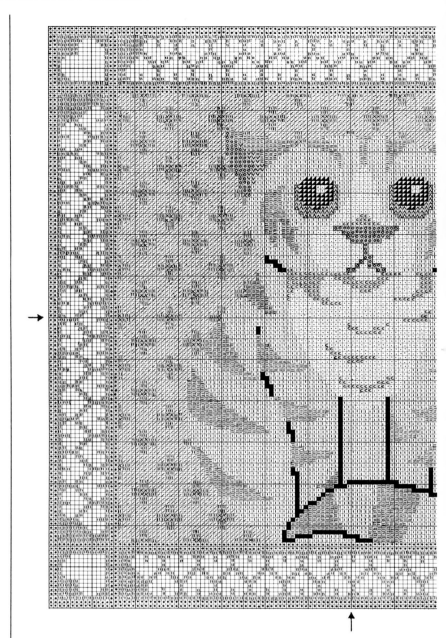

SUMMER ▲		DMC	ANCHOR	MADEIRA
☐	Bright canary yellow	973	290	0105
⬤	Dark royal blue	796	134	0914
‖	Red	666	46	0210
■	Dark golden brown	975	310	2303
Ɪ	Light topaz yellow	726	295	0109
•	White	White	2	White
C	Pale grey	415	398	1803
O	Very light peach	948	778	0306
⊟	Light pumpkin orange	970	316	0204
⊠	Medium lavender	210	109	0803
◤	Black	310	403	Black
⊽	Medium peach	352	9	0303
	Peach*	353	8	0304
⟁	Light yellowy green	3348	264	1409

Note: outline eyes in black and nose and mouth in peach (used
for backstitching only).*

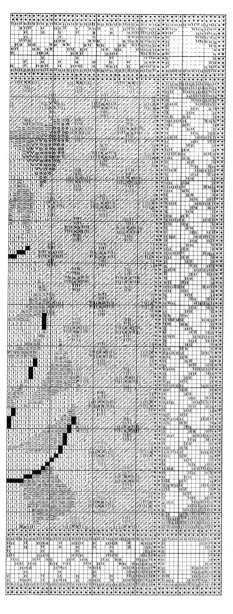

WINTER ▼		DMC	ANCHOR	MADEIRA
☐	Dark grey	413	401	1713
⦿	Light grey	318	399	1802
Ⅱ	Black	310	403	Black
☰	Very light avocado green	472	264	1414
◪	Dark forest green	986	245	1406
⊡	White	White	2	White
C	Pale grey	415	398	1803
◺	Very light peach	948	778	0306
.	Peach*	353	9	0304
☒	Medium peach	352	9	0303
⊙	Medium steel grey	317	400	1714
■	Very dark navy blue	939	152	1008
◣	Light yellowy green	3348	264	1409

Note: outline eyes in black and nose and mouth in peach* (used for backstitching only).

Butterflies

Decorated with butterflies, this sampler reminds one of sunny summer skies. The bright shades of pink in the centre are echoed in the floral border to continue the theme. Once again, part of the design could be omitted to add that personal touch. Your finished sampler will be like a breath of fresh air lifting the spirits. Stitch a feast for the eyes and revel in it!

BUTTERFLIES

YOU WILL NEED

For the Butterflies Sampler, with a design area measuring 22cm × 17.5cm (8½in × 7in), or 119 stitches by 97 stitches, here in a frame measuring 34cm × 30cm (13½in × 12in):

32cm × 27.5cm (12¾in × 11in) of white, 14-count Aida fabric
Stranded embroidery cotton in the colours given in the panel
No24 tapestry needle
Strong thread, for lacing across the back
Cardboard, for mounting, sufficient to fit into the frame recess
Frame of your choice

●

THE EMBROIDERY

Prepare the fabric and stretch it in a frame as explained on page 10. Following the chart, start the embroidery at the centre of the design, using two strands of embroidery cotton in the needle. Work each stitch over one block of fabric in each direction. Make sure that all the top crosses run in the same direction and each row is worked into the same holes as the top or bottom of the row before so that you do not leave a space between the rows.

Work the butterfly feelers in dark brown cotton, backstitching over two blocks of fabric.

MAKING UP

Gently steam press the work on the wrong side and mount it as explained on page 13. As this sampler has a rather bright modern feel about it, one of the floral-type frames might look attractive.

BUTTERFLIES ▶	DMC	ANCHOR	MADEIRA
% Light pink	605	50	0613
+ Dark pink	602	63	0702
✗ Yellow	3078	292	0102
c Light blue	932	920	1602
s Dark blue	311	148	1007
╱ Light green	3052	844	1509
: Dark green	3051	845	1508
= Light brown	841	378	1911
⟩ Dark brown	640	393	1905

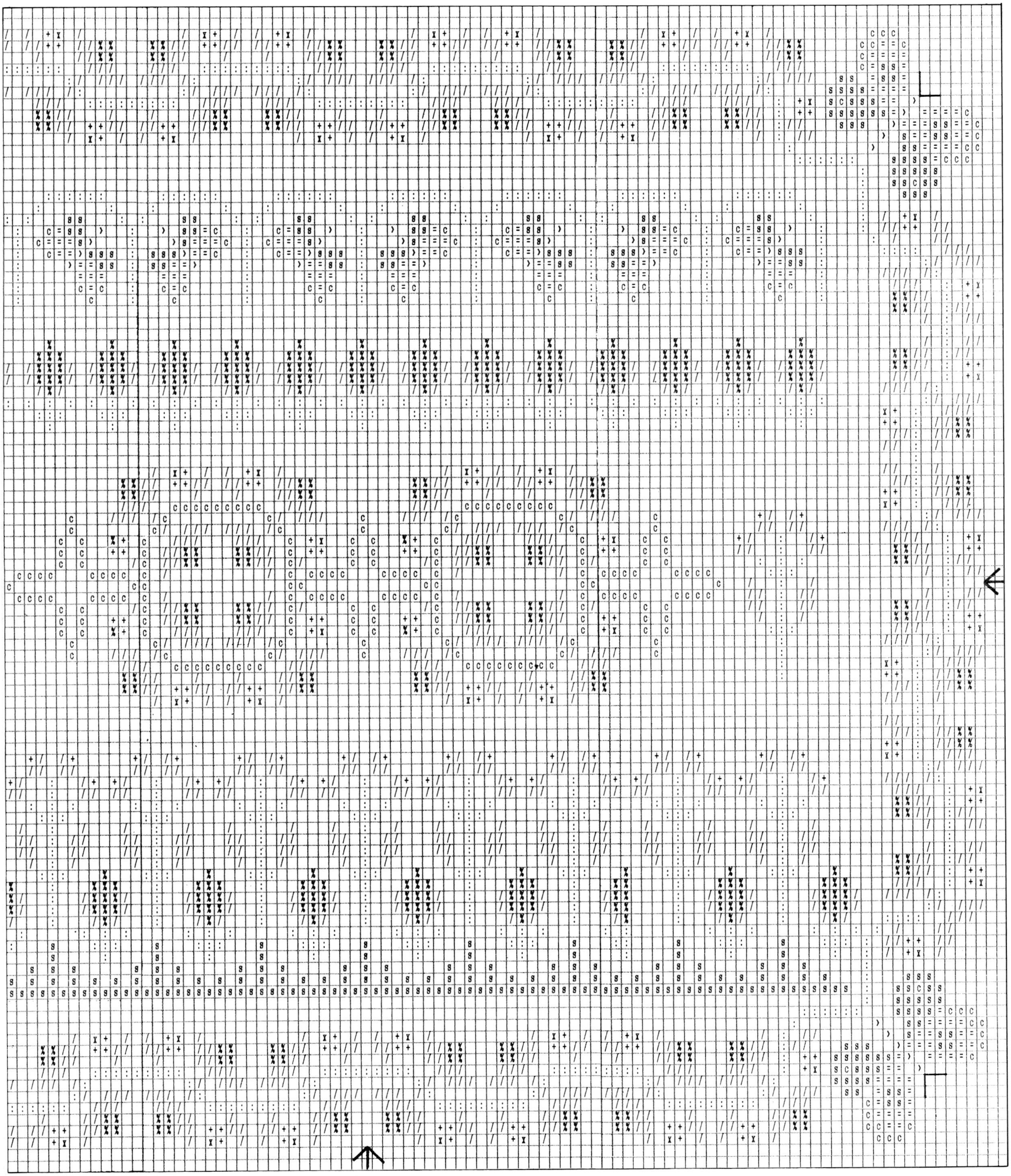

Nightdress Case

Make this luxurious case to tuck away your nightie or pyjamas during the day. Lightly padded, trimmed with ribbon bows, and featuring a sleeping cat, it will look beautiful sitting on top of any bed.

NIGHTDRESS CASE

YOU WILL NEED

For the Nightdress Case, measuring 45cm × 33cm
(17¾in × 13in):

*94cm × 46.5cm (37in × 18½in) of pink,
14-count Aida fabric
94cm × 46.5cm (37in × 18½in) of lightweight
polyester wadding
94cm × 46.5cm (37in × 18½in) of lightweight
cotton fabric for the lining
1.12m (44in) of ribbon, 2.5cm (1in) wide, in a
contrast colour
Stranded embroidery cotton in the colours given in
the panel
No 24 tapestry needle
Sewing thread to match the fabric*

•

THE EMBROIDERY

Prepare the edges of the fabric (see page 9); baste
a line across the width, 7.5cm (3in) up from the
bottom edge, to mark the baseline of the embroidery, and another 28.5cm (11½in) up from the
bottom edge (this marks off the area for the front
flap), then baste horizontal and vertical lines across
the embroidery area in the usual way.

Complete the cross stitching, working from the
centre and using two strands of embroidery thread
in the needle. Finish with the backstitching, made
with one thread in the needle. Gently steam press
the embroidery from the wrong side.

MAKING THE NIGHTDRESS CASE

Place the embroidered fabric face down on a flat
surface; carefully smooth the batting on top; pin
and baste the two together (12mm/½in seam
allowance); trim the batting back almost to the
basting line, and catch-stitch around the edge.

Make a single 12mm (½in) turning across the
width (not flap edge) of the fabric and baste. With
right sides facing, fold the pocket front section over
for 32cm (12½in); baste, and machine stitch to
form the pocket. Trim the corners and turn right
side out.

Make a single turning on the short edge of the
lining fabric and repeat as for the top fabric, but
do not turn the pocket to the right side.

With right sides of the top fabric and lining
together, baste and stitch around the flap, finishing

just above the side seams. Trim the corners and
turn the flap through to the right side. Slip the
lining into the pocket and slip stitch the top edges
together, easing the turning so that the stitching is
on the inside. Remove the basting stitches.

Cut the ribbon into two equal lengths; make two
bows and catch-stitch them to the flap of the nightdress case diagonally across the corners, as shown
in the photograph.

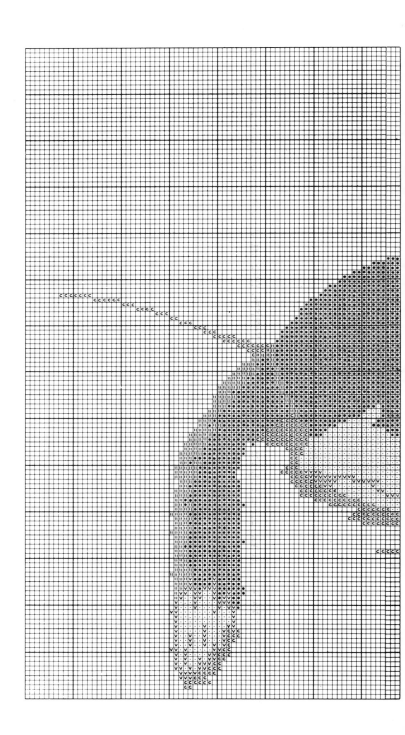

NIGHTDRESS			
CASE ▼	DMC	ANCHOR	MADEIRA
◢ Medium brick red	356	329	0402
● Black	310	403	Black
Ⅱ Medium steel grey	317	400	1714
∨ Pale grey	415	398	1803
• White	White	2	White
C Brown	3064	379	2310
✕ Light steel grey	318	399	1802
△ Steel grey	414	400	1801
P Peach	353	9	0304
⊟ Pale brick red	758	868	0403

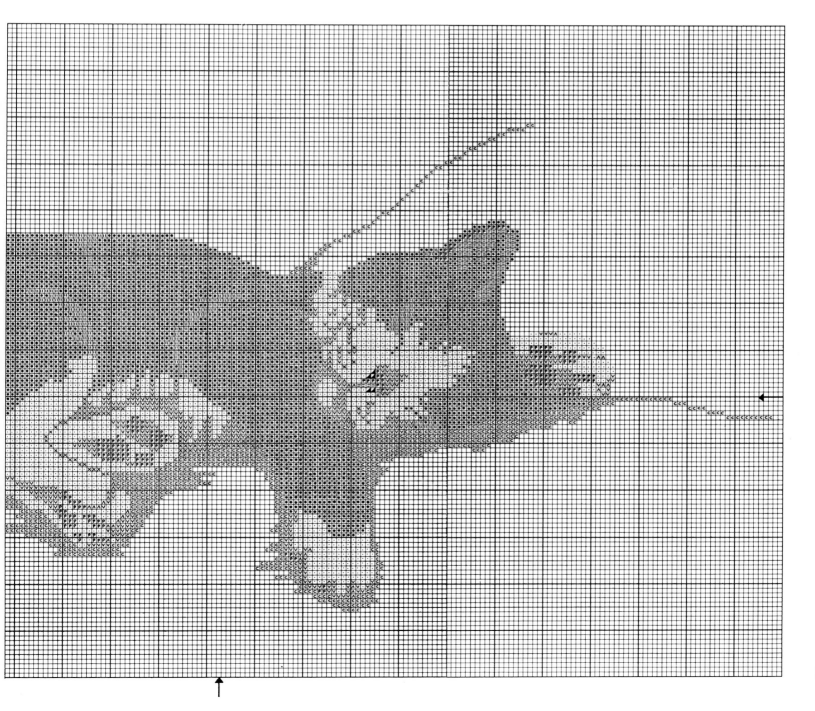

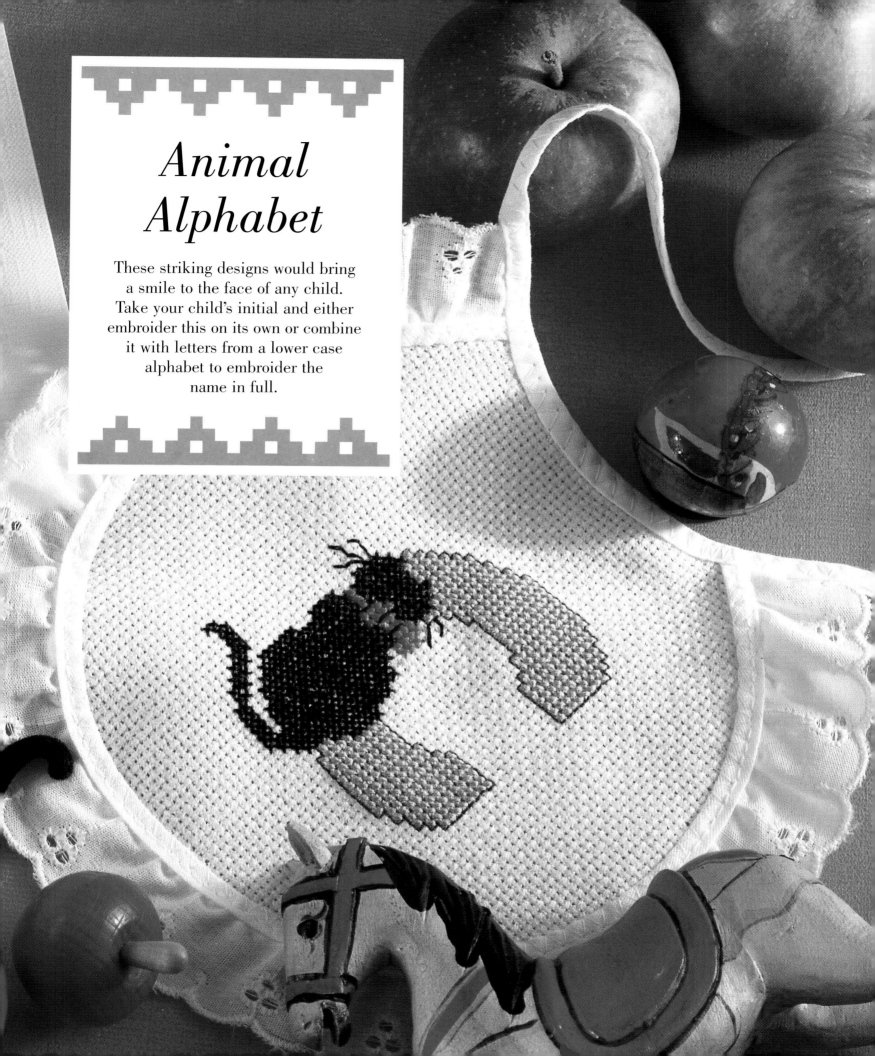

Animal Alphabet

These striking designs would bring a smile to the face of any child. Take your child's initial and either embroider this on its own or combine it with letters from a lower case alphabet to embroider the name in full.

ANIMAL ALPHABET

YOU WILL NEED

For the Card, measuring 20cm × 15cm
(8in × 6in), with an oval aperture measuring
15cm × 10cm (6in × 4in):

*25cm × 20cm (10in × 8in) of 14-count,
white Aida fabric
Stranded embroidery cotton in the colours given
in the panel
No24 tapestry needle
Card, for suppliers see page 220*

For the Framed Initial, here in a frame measuring
15cm × 11.5cm (6in × 4½in), with an aperture
measuring 13cm × 10cm (5¼in × 4in):

*20cm × 15cm (8in × 6in) of 14-count, white
Aida fabric
Stranded embroidery cotton in the colours given
in the panel
No24 tapestry needle
Frame of your choice*

**NOTE: *the letters vary in size, and the embroidery
for both the card and the picture can be worked on
virtually any count of evenweave fabric.***

For the Bib, measuring 18.5cm × 15cm
(7⅜in × 6in):

*Stranded embroidery cotton in the colours given
in the panel
No24 tapestry needle
Evenweave bib, for suppliers see page 220*

To embroider initials on purchased
(non-evenweave) clothes:

*Stranded embroidery cotton in the colours given
in the panel
No24 tapestry needle
Waste 14-count canvas,
a piece 5cm (2in) larger each way than the
dimensions of the finished embroidered initial
Fine tweezers
Water spray
Basting cotton and needle
Chosen item of clothing*

CARD

Prepare the fabric, marking the centre with horizontal and vertical lines of basting stitches. Mount it in a hoop as explained on page 9. Start the stitching at the centre, using two strands of cotton in the needle, if using 14-count Aida (see Stitching details). Take each stitch over one block of fabric in each direction, making sure that all the top crosses run in the same direction and that each row is worked into the same holes as the top or bottom of the row before, so that you do not leave a space between rows.

MAKING UP

Gently steam press the embroidery on the wrong side and trim it to measure 12mm (½in) larger each way than the aperture. Centre your embroidery behind the opening and secure it in place with double-sided tape. Press the card firmly together.

FRAMED INITIAL

The embroidery is worked in the same way as for the card. Gently steam press the finished embroidery on the wrong side; mount it (see page 13), and set it in a frame of your choice.

THE BIB

Mark the centre of the bib with horizontal and vertical lines of basting stitches, and embroider your chosen initial (see individual stitching details), using two strands of embroidery cotton in the needle and taking each stitch over one block of the fabric.

When you have finished, remove the basting stitches and gently steam press the bib on the wrong side.

USING WASTE CANVAS

Position the blue threads of the canvas horizontally or vertically with the weave of the garment. Pin and then baste the canvas in place and remove the pins. Each pair of canvas threads is treated as one thread, so the cross stitch is worked over one pair of threads in each direction. Start stitching in the centre, which you can mark on the canvas with a vertical and horizontal line of basting stitches. Begin the embroidery by fastening the cotton with your first stitches, and finish by threading the cotton through a few stitches at the back of the work. Make sure that you start and finish firmly, so that the stitches do not pull out during washing.

When the cross stitching is complete, trim the

canvas to within 12mm (½in) of the embroidery. Dampen the embroidery on the right side with warm water and leave for a few minutes until the threads soften. Using tweezers, pull the canvas threads out one at a time so that you do not damage your embroidery.

Press the embroidery by placing it right side down on a towel and pressing with a hot iron and damp cloth.

ALPHABET STITCHING DETAILS

All letters are worked using three strands of stranded cotton for 11-count fabric, two for 14-count fabric and one for 18- or 22-count fabric.

All outlining is in backstitch, using one strand of dark grey unless stated otherwise. Additional stitching details are as follows:

The letter B
Embroider the bee's wings in backstitch with one strand of dark grey.

The letter C
Embroider the whiskers in backstitch with two strands of black cotton.

The letters E and J
Embroider the water in backstitch with two strands of dark blue.

The letter I
Embroider the feelers in backstitch, using two strands of black cotton.

The letter L
Embroider the feelers in backstitch, using two strands of black cotton.

The letter R
Embroider the whiskers in backstitch with one strand of dark grey cotton.

The letter S
Embroider the whiskers in straight stitch with one strand of black cotton.

The letter U
Embroider the tufts of hair in backstitch with two strands of yellow cotton.

The letter V
Embroider the vipers' tongue in backstitch, using two strands of black cotton.

The letter W
Embroider the water in backstitch with two strands of pale blue.

ANIMAL ALPHABET		DMC	ANCHOR	MADEIRA
C	Light gold	676	887	2208
V	Dark gold	729	890	2209
/	Light brown	437	362	2011
=	Medium brown	435	(363)	2009
Z	Dark brown	434	365	2008
X	Moss green	471	265	(1501)
S	Light jade green	563	208	1207
W	Dark jade green	562	210	(1206)
r	Red	349	(46)	0212
·	Yellow	743	301	0109
e	Light blue	800	128	1014
n	Dark blue	799	130	1012
+	Light grey	318	235	1802
>	Medium grey	414	399	1801
–	Pink	604	60	(0614)
a	Mauve	340	118	0902
*	Black	Black	403	Black
0	White	White	1	White
	Dark grey*	3799	(236)	(1713)

Note: numbers in brackets indicate the nearest colour match; for backstitched outline use dark grey* (used for bks only).

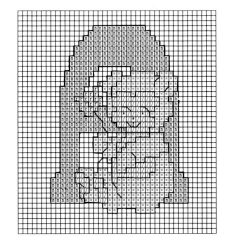

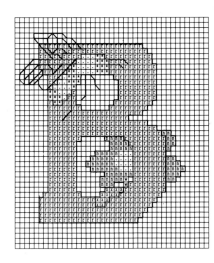

Turn to page 168 for charts for the remaining letters.

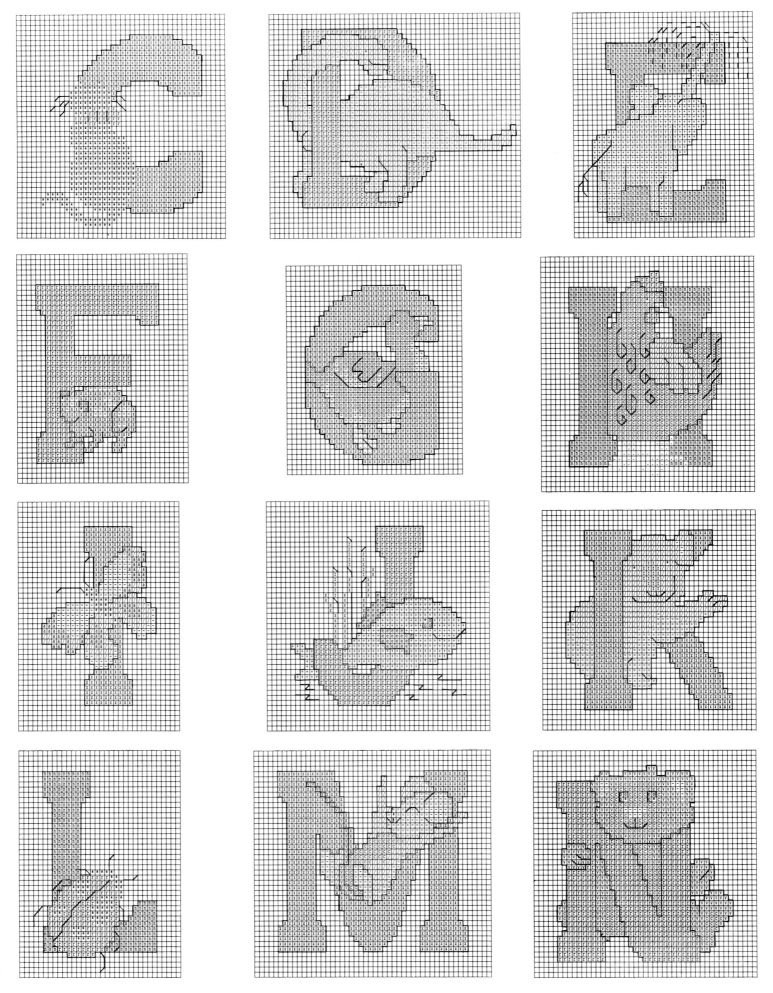

TEDDIES
TO
TREASURE

Teddy bears, those most endearing and
enduring of toys, are the subject of
this chapter. You will find them
adorning cushions, pictures, cards and
even a toy bag – pure indulgence for teddy
lovers of all ages!

CUDDLY CUSHIONS

YOU WILL NEED

For each Cushion, measuring 25cm (10in) square,
excluding lace edging:

35cm (14in) square of white, 14-count Aida fabric
27.5cm (11in) square of contrast fabric,
to back your cushion
2.4m (2⅔yds) of white lace edging,
4cm (1½in) deep
Stranded embroidery cotton in the colours given
in the appropriate panel
Matching sewing thread
No24 tapestry needle
27.5cm (11in) square cushion pad

THE EMBROIDERY

Prepare the fabric, marking the centre lines of the
design with basting stitches, and mount it in a hoop
or frame, following the instructions on page 9.
Referring to the appropriate chart, complete the
cross stitching, starting at the centre and using two
strands in the needle throughout. Embroider the
main areas first, and then finish with the backstitching, this time using a single strand in the
needle. Steam press on the wrong side.

MAKING UP THE COVER

Trim the embroidery to measure 27.5cm (11in)
square. Using a tiny french seam, join the short
edges of the lace together. Run a gathering thread
close to the straight edge; pull up the gathers to fit
and, with the right side of the embroidery facing and
the lace lying on the fabric, baste the edging to the

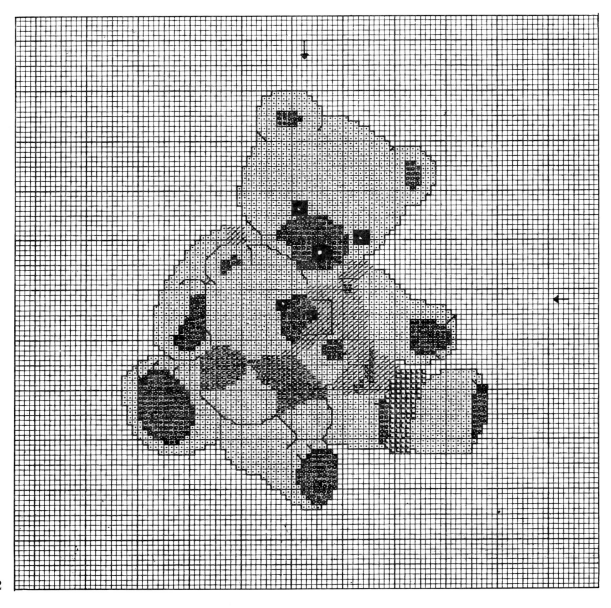

172

outer edge, placing it just inside the 12mm (½in) seam allowance. Adjust the gathers evenly, allowing a little extra fullness at the corners. Machine stitch the frill in place.

With right sides together, place the backing fabric on top; baste and machine stitch around, leaving a 20cm (8in) opening in the middle of one side. Remove basting stitches; trim across the corners, and turn the cover through. Insert the cushion pad and slip stitch the opening to secure it.

FATHER AND SON ◄	DMC	ANCHOR	MADEIRA
☐ White	White	2	White
C Christmas red	321	47	0510
V Garnet red	815	43	0513
L Baby blue	3325	159	1002
X Medium navy	311	148	1006
╱ Dark baby blue	322	978	1004
O Pale golden wheat	3047	886	2205
Z Medium topaz	782	307	2212
• Tan	436	363	2011
Dark coffee*	801	357	2007*
■ Black	310	403	Black

Note: dark coffee* used to backstitch around bodies, dark baby blue for trouser leg, medium navy for other clothing.

MOTHER AND DAUGHTER ▼	DMC	ANCHOR	MADEIRA
☐ White	White	2	White
╱ Pink	3326	26	0504
• Dark pink	335	42	0506
C Medium lavender	210	104	0802
‖ Dark lavender	208	110	0804
O Pale golden wheat	3047	886	2205
• Tan	436	363	2011
Dark coffee*	801	357	2007*
Light grey*	415	398	1803
■ Black	310	403	Black

Note: dark coffee* used to backstitch around bodies, light grey* for sleeve.

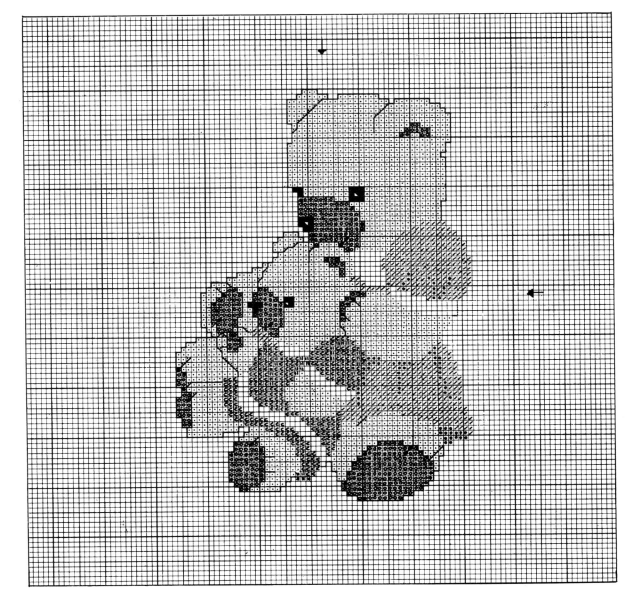

Teddy Bear Cards

A personalized greetings card containing a small embroidery is a pleasure to make and a way of showing that the recipient is special.

TEDDY BEAR CARDS

YOU WILL NEED

For each Card, measuring 15.5cm × 11cm
(6¼in × 4in):

*19cm × 15cm (7½in × 6in) of white, 22-count
Hardanger fabric
Stranded embroidery cotton in the colours given in
the appropriate panel
No26 tapestry needle
Double-sided adhesive tape
Card mount (for suppliers, see page 220)
as appropriate:
Christmas Bear card – holly green with round
inner frame, 8cm (3in) in diameter
Birthday Bear card – pale blue with round
inner frame 8cm (3in) in diameter
Valentine Bear card – Christmas red with oval
inner frame, 10.5cm × 8cm (4½in × 3in)
Iron-on interfacing (optional – see Making up the
cards) – 12mm larger all-round than the size of
the inner frame of the chosen card*

•

THE EMBROIDERY

All three cards are stitched in the same way and
on the same type of fabric.

Note that it is particularly important with
embroidered cards to avoid excessive overstitching
on the back, as this would cause unsightly lumps
to show through on the right side.

Prepare the fabric, marking the centre lines of
each design with basting stitches, and mount it in
a small hoop, following the instructions on page 6.
Referring to the appropriate chart, complete the
cross stitching, using a single strand in the needle
throughout. Embroider the main areas first, and
then finish with the backstitching. If necessary,
steam press on the wrong side.

It is a good idea to leave the basting stitches in
at this stage, as they will prove useful in helping to
centre your design in the card window.

MAKING UP THE CARDS

It is not strictly necessary to use iron-on interfacing,
but it helps to avoid wrinkles. If you are using interfacing, place it on the back of the embroidery; use a
pencil to mark the basting/registration points on
the interfacing and outer edge of the embroidery.

Remove basting stitches and iron the interfacing in
place, aligning marks.

Trim the embroidery to about 12mm (½in) larger
than the cut-out window, and then, making sure that
the motif is placed in the middle by measuring an
equal distance at each side of the marks, position the
embroidery behind the window. Use double-sided
tape to fix the embroidery into the card, then press
the backing down firmly.

BIRTHDAY ▼		DMC	ANCHOR	MADEIRA
□	White	White	2	White
ΙΙ	Medium pink	899	27	0505
x	Deep rose	309	42	0507
c	Delft blue	809	130	0909
	Royal blue*	797	132	0912
Ι	Light tan	738	942	2013
•	Light brown	434	309	2009
	Very dark coffee*	898	360	2006
■	Black	310	403	Black

Note: black used to backstitch around the mouth, very dark coffee for
bear, royal blue* (starred colours are used for bks only) for ribbon.*

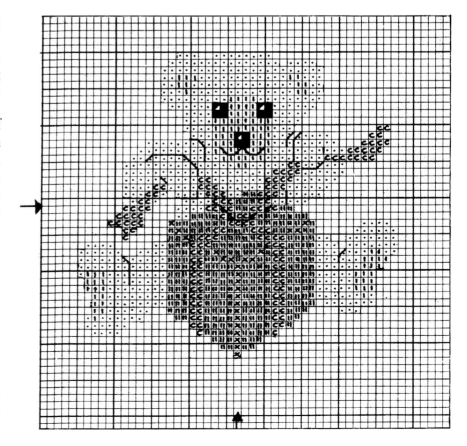

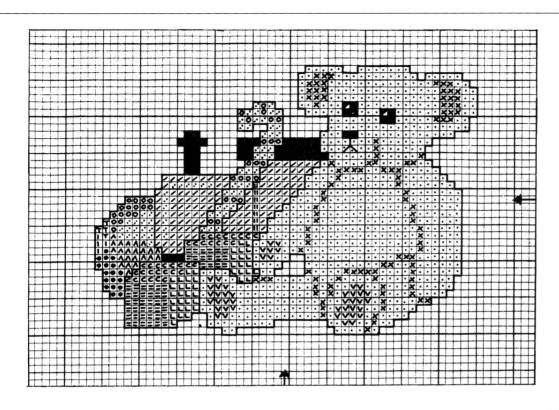

CHRISTMAS ▲		DMC	ANCHOR	MADEIRA
.·	White	White	2	White
c	Pink	3326	26	0504
o	Bright red	666	46	0210
L	Dark lavender	208	110	0804
●	Light pumpkin	970	316	0204
x	Medium tangerine	741	304	0201
·	Dark yellow	743	297	0113
Λ	Medium bright blue	996	433	1103
=	Delft blue	809	130	0909
T	Dark blue	825	162	1011
I	Light emerald	912	209	1212
/	Light green	989	256	1401
II	Dark green	987	245	1403
V	Medium gold brown	976	309	2302
	Very dark grey*	844	401	1810
■	Black	310	403	Black

Note: very dark grey* used for bks outlines, and black for mouth.

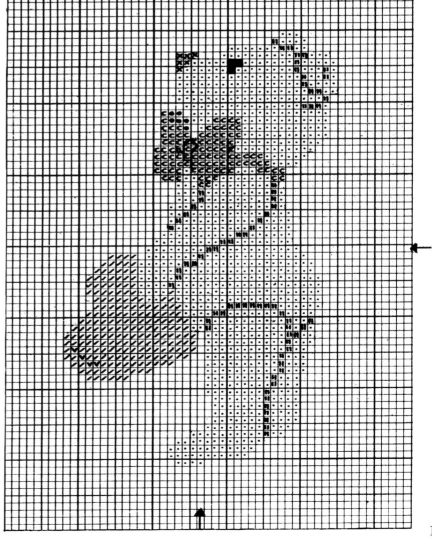

VALENTINE ▶		DMC	ANCHOR	MADEIRA
v	White	White	2	White
/	Red	349	13	0212
c	Medium baby blue	334	161	1003
●	Light navy	312	147	1005
	Medium navy*	311	148	1006
·	Medium old gold	729	907	2209
II	Dark topaz brown	781	308	2213
x	Dark coffee	801	357	2007
■	Black	310	403	Black

Note: medium navy* used for bks ribbon.

A Picture for Baby

This charming picture would certainly win the heart of anyone with a newborn baby. Traditionalists will no doubt sew the letters in blue for a boy, or pink for a girl.

A PICTURE FOR BABY

YOU WILL NEED

For the Picture, measuring 50cm × 24cm
(20in × 9½), unframed:

*58.5cm × 31.5cm (23in × 12½in) of white,
14-count Aida fabric*
*Stranded embroidery cotton in the colours given
in the panel; two skeins of tan are required, and
three of either baby blue or pale dusty rose*
*50cm × 24cm (20in × 9½in) of firm cardboard,
for a mount*
*50cm × 24cm (20in × 9½in) of iron-on
interfacing (optional – see Mounting the picture)*
No24 tapestry needle
Picture frame of your choice

THE EMBROIDERY

Prepare the fabric, marking the centre lines of the
design with basting stitches, and mount it in a
frame, following the instructions on page 7. Referring to the chart, complete the cross stitching,
using three strands in the needle throughout.
Embroider the main areas first, and then finish with
the backstitching, this time using two strands of
thread in the needle. If necessary, steam press on
the wrong side.

It is a good idea to leave the basting stitches in at
this stage, as they will prove useful in helping to
centre your design on the mount.

MOUNTING THE PICTURE

Take care that your working surface is absolutely
clean and dry. If you wish to use an iron-on interfacing, to help to avoid wrinkles, iron this to the back
of the embroidery, following the same procedure as
for the cards on page 176. If you are not using interfacing, leave the basting stitches in place and
remove them after mounting.
Mount your picture on the firm cardboard, following the instructions given for heavier fabrics. Mark
the centre of the board at the top, bottom and sides,
and match centre marks for accurate alignment.

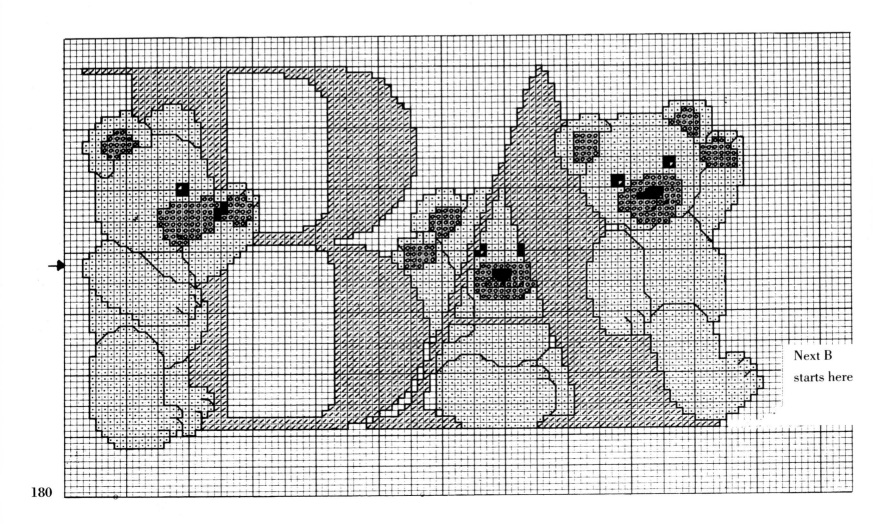

Next B
starts here

PICTURE FOR BABY	DMC	ANCHOR	MADEIRA
△ White	White	2	White
╱ Baby blue	3325	159	1002
Dark baby blue*	322	978	1004
╱ Pale dusty rose	963	48	0608
Dark dusty rose*	961	40	0610
○ Pale golden wheat	3047	886	2205
· Tan	436	363	2011
Medium brown*	433	371	2008
■ Black	310	403	Black

Note: outline pale golden wheat with medium brown*, baby blue with dark baby blue* or pale dusty rose with dark dusty rose* (starred colours are used for backstitching only); use either baby blues (for a boy) or dusty pinks (for a girl); two skeins needed of tan, and three of either baby blue or pale dusty rose.

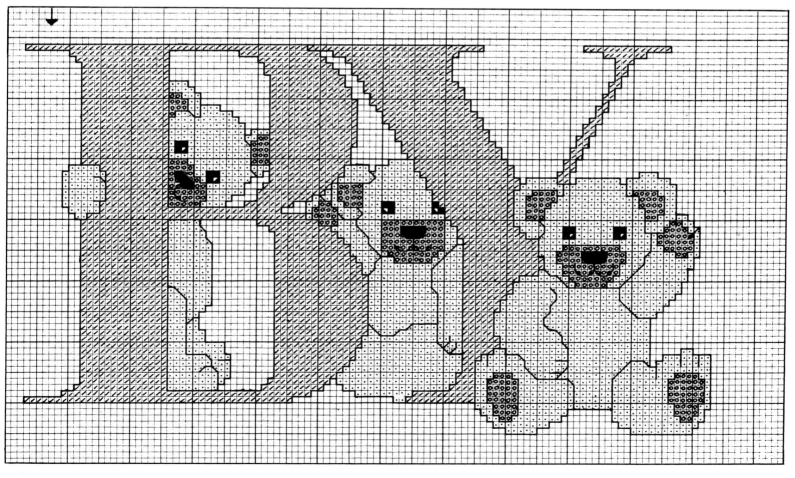

Baby's Coverlet

Could any tiny child, or mother, resist the enchantment of these lovely sleepy teddies? This wonderfully soft and practical Afghan fabric, featuring 13cm (5in) squares, is ideal for a baby's coverlet, and easily washable.

BABY'S COVERLET

YOU WILL NEED

For a Coverlet, measuring 86cm × 104cm
(34in × 41in):

92cm × 110cm (37in × 44in) of
Anne Afghan fabric
Stranded embroidery cotton in the colours given in
the panel; two skeins of tan are required
Matching cream sewing thread
No26 tapestry needle

•

THE EMBROIDERY

Following the diagram, cut the fabric to size. If you
are securing the fringe by machine, stitch a zigzag
border all around, as indicated. Mark the centre
lines of each design with basting stitches, and
mount the fabric in a hoop, following the instructions on page 9. Referring to the appropriate chart,
complete each design, starting at the centre of each
and using two strands in the needle for cross stitching and one for backstitched lines.

COMPLETING THE COVERLET

Trim the fabric to the final size. To make the fringe,
either remove fabric threads one at a time until you
reach the zigzag stitch line, or hemstitch, as shown.
Brush out the fringe with a stiff brush.

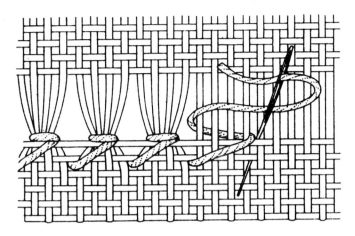

HEMSTITCH

Remove a single thread from the fabric at the hem-
line (the start of the fringe). Bring the needle out on
the right side, two threads below the drawn-thread
line. Working from left to right, pick up either two or
three threads, as shown in the diagram. Bring the
needle out again and insert it behind the fabric, to
emerge two threads down, ready to make the next
stitch. Before reinserting the needle, pull the thread
tight, so that the bound threads form a neat group. To
complete the fringe, remove the weft threads below
the hemstitching.

Final cutting line   Final cutting line

Final cutting line

Zigzag border

Final cutting line

Design 1

Design 2   Design 2

Design 1

Design 3   Design 3

104cm (41in)

86cm (34in)

BABY'S COVERLET ▶		DMC	ANCHOR	MADEIRA
L	White	White	2	White
∴	Medium lavender	210	104	0802
●	Dark carnation	891	29	0411
I	Delft blue	809	130	0909
X	Light emerald	912	209	1212
╱	Very light yellow	3078	292	0102
O	Light topaz	727	293	0110
c	Very light brown	435	365	2010
V	Light brown	434	309	2009
•	Tan	436	363	2011
∧	Light grey	415	398	1803
	Steel grey*	317	400	1714
	Dark steel grey*	413	401	1713
	Black*	310	403	Black

Note: black* used for bks clock hands, clock numbers steel grey*,
all outlines dark steel grey*.

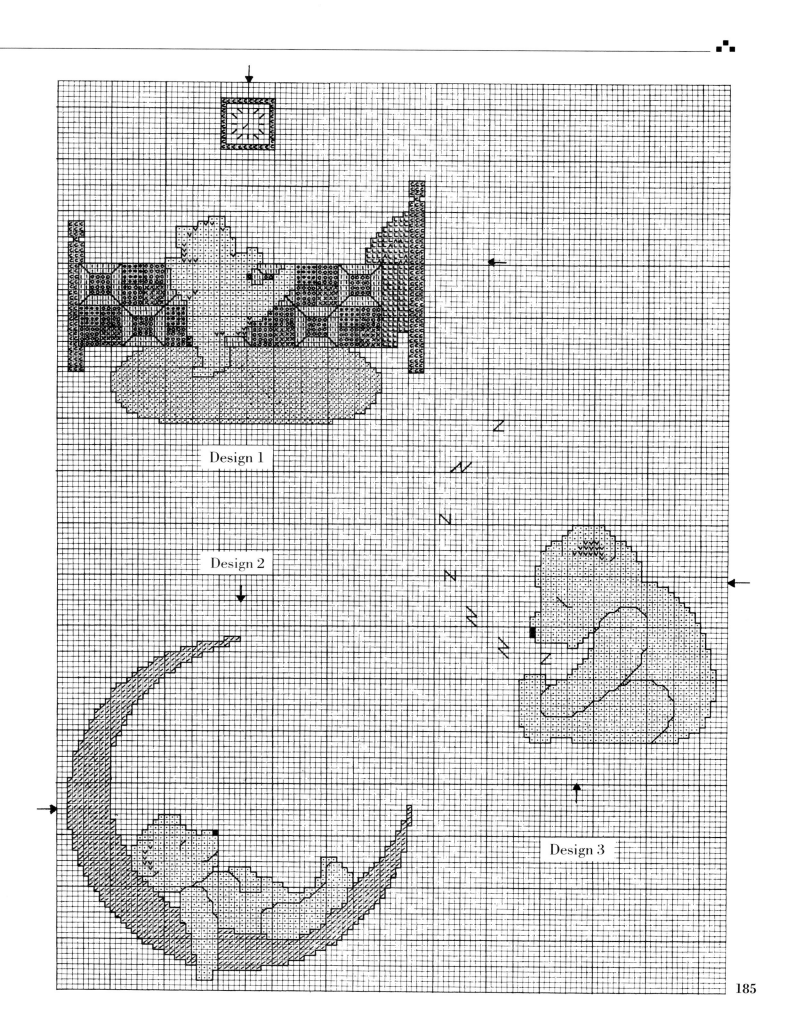

Design 1

Design 2

Design 3

Toy Bag

Suitable for a child of any age group, this toy bag will make an extremely practical gift, and a bright and attractive feature in the playroom or nursery. The bag has a draw-string top and is both large enough and strong enough to hold many small toys.

TOY BAG

YOU WILL NEED

For the Toy Bag, measuring 60cm × 44cm
(24in × 17½):

*65cm (26in) of cream pearl Aida fabric, 110cm
(43in) wide, with 11 threads to 2.5cm (1in)
65cm (26in) of firm, unbleached cotton (calico),
110cm (43in) wide, for the lining
250cm (2½yds) of white cord, 6mm (¼in)
in diameter
Stranded embroidery cotton in the colours
given in the panel
Matching sewing thread
No24 tapestry needle*

•

THE EMBROIDERY

Take a piece of fabric measuring 65cm × 50cm
(26in × 20in). Prepare the fabric, marking the
centre lines of the design with basting stitches;
ensure that there is a clearance around the design
area of 15.5cm (6½in) at the sides and bottom, and
26cm (10¼in) at the top, and mount it in a hoop
or frame, following the instructions on page 9.
Referring to the chart, complete the cross stitching,
using three strands in the needle throughout.
Embroider the main areas first, and then finish with
the backstitching, this time using two strands of
thread in the needle. If necessary, steam press on
the wrong side.

MAKING THE BAG

Trim the edges of the embroidered fabric until the
piece measures 47cm × 63.5cm (18½in × 25in),
with a clearance around the design of 14cm (5½in)
at the sides and bottom and 25.5cm (10in) from the
top. Cut a second piece of Aida fabric to match.

With right sides together and taking a 12mm
(½in) seam allowance, stitch the side seams,
stitching down from the top for 5cm (2in), leaving a
gap of 3.5cm (1¼in), and then continuing to the
bottom (A).

Join the bottom seam. Press the seams flat and
topstitch around each gap, 6mm (¼in) from the
pressed edge, as shown (B).

Cut two lining pieces, each measuring 47cm ×
62.5cm (18½in × 24½in). Place the two pieces of
lining fabric with right sides together and stitch the

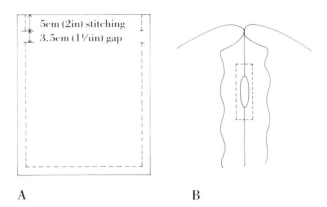

A   B

side seams (all the way), and then the bottom seam,
leaving an opening of 15cm (6in) for turning (C).

Place the outer bag into the lining, with right sides
together, and stitch around the top edge. Press
seams flat, then turn the bag right side out through
the opening. Slip stitch the opening to close it. Press
around the top of the bag, then topstitch two lines,
6mm (¼in) above and below the side openings (D).
Thread the cord twice through the resulting case-
ment and tie the ends together.

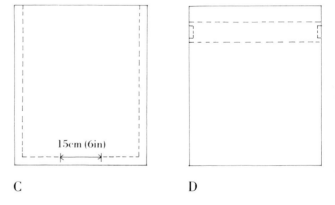

C   D

TOY BAG ▶		DMC	ANCHOR	MADEIRA
□	White	White	2	White
v	Garnet	816	20	0512
ᴸ	Dark Christmas red	498	47	0511
–	Lemon yellow	307	289	0104
T	Christmas gold	783	307	2211
\	Tangerine	740	316	0202
╱	Bright orange	606	335	0209
∧	Baby blue	3325	159	1002
=	Medium baby blue	334	161	1003
C	Dark baby blue	322	978	1004
X	Aquamarine	992	187	1202
●	Royal blue	797	132	0912
H	Medium navy	311	148	1006
‖	Dark emerald	910	228	1310
O	Very light tan	738	942	2013
•	Tan	436	363	2011
•	Medium topaz	782	307	2212
z	Light brown	434	309	2009
L	Dark coffee	801	357	2007
	Very dark beaver*	844	401	1810
■	Black	310	403	Black

Note: very dark beaver* used for all backstitch outlines.

CHRISTMAS BLESSINGS

Christmas stitching remains as popular as ever, and this small collection of seasonal designs will add a festive touch to any home. Stitch up your Christmas with a range of Christmas cards, crackers, tree decorations, and even a Yuletide cake band!

A SPECIAL TIME OF YEAR

YOU WILL NEED

For the Picture, set in a 12.5cm × 17.5cm
(5in × 7in) frame:

*20cm × 25cm (8in × 10in) of antique white,
28-count Monaco evenweave fabric
Stranded embroidery cotton in the colours given
in the panel
No26 tapestry needle
Strong thread, for lacing across the back
Cross-over wooden frame (for suppliers, see page 220)*

*NOTE: Monaco fabric, from Charles Craft, USA, is
available from many needlework shops and suppliers,
but if you cannot obtain this fabric, use any 28-count
evenweave linen fabric.*

•

THE EMBROIDERY

Prepare the fabric as described on page 9; find the
centre by folding, and mark the horizontal and
vertical centre lines with basting stitches in a light-
coloured thread. Set the fabric in a frame or hoop
(see page 9) and count out from the centre to start
stitching at a point convenient to you.

Work all cross stitching first and then the half
crosses, using two strands of thread in the needle.
Take the stitches over two fabric threads, ensuring
that all top stitches lie in the same direction. Finish
with the backstitching, using one strand of thread in
the needle.

ASSEMBLING THE PICTURE

When the design is completed, gently handwash the
finished piece, if necessary, then press lightly on the
wrong side, using a cool iron. Mark the central
horizontal and vertical lines on the back of the
mount provided and, matching these with the central
basting stitches, lace the embroidery over the
mount, following the instructions on page 13.
Carefully remove the basting stitches.

Insert the embroidery into the frame, according to
the manufacturer's instructions (a framing mount has
not been used with this design).

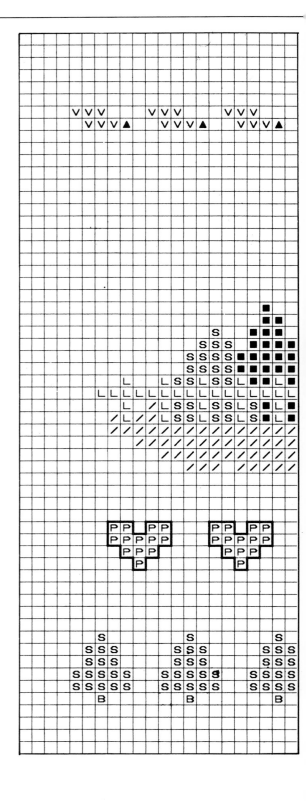

A SPECIAL TIME OF YEAR ▲   DMC ANCHOR MADEIRA   DMC ANCHOR MADEIRA

Cross	Half Cross		DMC	ANCHOR	MADEIRA
S		Clear green	3363	262	1602
B		Medium golden brown	611	898	2107
P		Medium salmon pink	760	9	0405
▲		Pink red	3328	1024	0406
L		Light golden brown	612	832	2108
■		Dark green	520	862	1514
V		Medium blue green	502	876	1703
I		Dark beige grey	3022	392	1903
T		Light tan brown	437	362	2012
C		Medium brown grey	640	903	1905

Cross	Half Cross		DMC	ANCHOR	MADEIRA
\		Light beige brown	842	376	1910
=		Medium beige grey	3023	899	1902
G		Medium gold	676	891	2208
	/	Pale silver grey	762	397	1804
		Dark golden brown*	610	905	1914

Note: bks house outline and window panes in dark golden brown* (used for backstitch only), bow in pink red, and wreath on door in dark green. Use on strand of pink red to make tiny french knots on the wreath on the front door.

Christmas Cards

Personalized greetings cards containing a small embroidery are a pleasure to make or receive. Christmas cards first became popular in the late Victorian era. Early cards were decorated with flowers, then came the more traditional Christmas themes, such as holly, robins and snow scenes, followed by nativities and angels.

CHRISTMAS CARDS

YOU WILL NEED

For each Card, the large cards measuring
16cm × 11cm (6¼in × 4¼in), and the small
cards 9cm × 12cm (3¼in × 4½in):

*Stranded embroidery cotton in the colours given in
the appropriate panel
No26 tapestry needle
Double-sided adhesive tape
Appropriate card, as listed below (for suppliers, see
page 220)*

•

For the *Bethlehem* card:

9cm × 12cm (3¼in × 4½in) of sky blue,
22-count Hardanger
Small Christmas red card with a rectangular
cut-out

For the *Santa* card:

9cm × 12cm (3¼in × 4½in) of silver fleck,
20-count Bellana fabric
Small Christmas red card with a rectangular
cut-out

For the *Robins* card:

16cm × 11cm (6¼in × 4¼in) of silver fleck,
20-count Bellana fabric
Large Christmas red card with an oval cut-out

For the *Nöel* card:

16cm × 11cm (6¼in × 4¼in) of white, 18-count
Aida fabric
Large holly green card with a rectangular cut-out

For the *Xmas* card:

16cm × 11cm (6¼in × 4¼in) of silver fleck,
20-count Bellana fabric
Large holly green card with a circular cut-out

For the *Shepherd* card:

16cm × 11cm (6¼in × 4¼in) of white, 20-count
Bellana fabric
Large holly green card with an oval cut-out

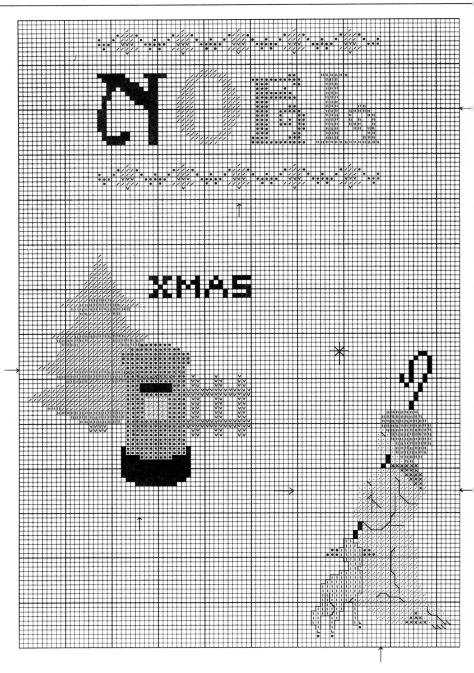

THE EMBROIDERY

Each card is made in the same way. To economize
on fabric, you could make the *Santa, Robins,* and
Xmas cards on a single piece of fabric, providing
you leave sufficient space around each design.

Prepare the fabric, marking the centre (of each
design, if you are stitching several on a single
piece) with horizontal and vertical lines of basting
stitches (see page 9). Set the fabric in a hoop, and
complete the cross stitch embroidery, using one
strand of embroidery cotton in the needle throughout. When you have completed the embroidery,
gently press the finished piece from the wrong side,
leaving the basting stitches in postition at this stage.

NÖEL ◄		DMC	ANCHOR	MADEIRA
⊙	Dark Kelly green	701	227	1305
⟋	Topaz yellow	725	306	0108
⌄	Medium topaz yellow	782	307	2212
■	Bright Christmas red	666	46	0210
⥠	Dark violet	552	100	0713

XMAS ◄		DMC	ANCHOR	MADEIRA
■	Black	310	403	Black
⟋	Kelly green	702	226	0306
⥠	Christmas green	699	923	1303
⌄	Medium brown	433	371	2008
⊠	Dark Christmas red	498	47	0511
⊙	Light red	350	11	0213
⦂	White	White	2	White

SHEPHERD ◄		DMC	ANCHOR	MADEIRA
■	Medium brown	433	371	2008
⥠	Very light brown	435	365	2010
⦁	Light peach	754	6	0305
	Medium peach*	352	9	0303
⊠	Dark antique mauve	315	896	0810
⦂	Antique mauve	316	894	0809
⊟	White	White	2	White
⊙	Black	310	403	Black
⌊	Light steel grey	318	399	1802
	Silver thread*	—	—	—

Note: bks around light peach with medium peach*; white with light steel grey, and star with silver thread* (starred colours used for bks only).

BETHLEHEM ►		DMC	ANCHOR	MADEIRA
⊙	Silver thread	—	—	—
■	Black	310	403	Black
⦁	White	White	2	White
⟋	Light peach	754	6	0305
⥠	Dark aqua	958	187	1114
⌊	Light steel grey	318	399	1802
⌄	Light loden green	3364	843	1512
⊠	Dark loden green	3362	846	1514

SANTA ►		DMC	ANCHOR	MADEIRA
■	Bright Christmas red	666	46	0210
⦁	Light peach	754	6	0305
⦂	White	White	2	White
	Light steel grey*	318	399	1802
⥠	Kelly green	702	226	0306
⊙	Black	310	403	Black
⌄	Medium peach	352	9	0303

Note: bks string in black; around white with light steel grey* (used for bks only), and around light peach with medium peach.

ROBINS ►		DMC	ANCHOR	MADEIRA
⦂	Pale grey	415	398	1803
■	Black	310	403	Black
⊙	Dark forest brown	938	381	2005
⟋	Medium brown	433	371	2008
⦁	Medium yellow	744	301	0112
Ⓞ	Very light mahogany brown	402	347	2307
⥠	Light red	350	11	0213

MAKING UP THE CARDS

Trim the embroidery to measure slightly larger all around than the card window, then centre it behind the window, using the basting stitches as guidelines. Make light pencil marks on the back of the embroidery and the back of the window, to act as registration marks. Remove the basting stitches, then replace the card in the window. Use double-sided tape to secure the card in position, then press the backing down firmly.

A Victorian Christmas

The Victorian era provides the theme for these richly-coloured ornaments. Inserted into small frames, they would prove ideal for hanging on a tree, but the same motifs could be used for greeting cards, gift tags, or the placecards on your Christmas dinner table.

A VICTORIAN CHRISTMAS

YOU WILL NEED

For each Motif, set in a frame measuring 6.5cm (2½in) in diameter:

Approximately 10cm (4in) square of ivory, 18-count Aida fabric
Stranded embroidery cotton in the colours given in the appropriate panel
Balger blending filament in gold, one spool
No26 tapestry needle
Approximately 20cm (8in) of ribbon, 6mm (¼in) wide, optional, for a bow
Round gold-coloured frame, for suppliers see page 220

NOTE: if you are stitching all the motifs, you will only need one skein of each colour.

•

THE EMBROIDERY

Each design uses only a small amount of fabric, and to avoid any waste you may prefer to embroider designs in batches. For each motif, prepare the fabric as described on page 9, and mark the horizontal and vertical centre lines with basting stitches in a light-coloured thread. Set the fabric in a hoop and count out from the centre to start stitching at a point convenient to you. Work all cross stitches first, making sure that all top stitches run in the same direction. Finally, work all backstitch details.

Use one strand of embroidery cotton in the needle when making cross stitches and half-stitches, and also for backstitching. Gently handwash the finished piece, if necessary, and lightly press with a steam iron on the wrong side.

ASSEMBLY

Use the clear plastic from the frame to trim the embroidery to a size that will fit in the frame. Centre the design in the frame, and carefully push in the snap-in back. Trim with a ribbon bow, if desired.

VICTORIAN BOW ▶		DMC	ANCHOR	MADEIRA
P	Dark salmon	760	9	0405
O	Light pink red	3328	11	0406
	Dark red*	347	19	0407
X	Apple green	320	216	1311
L	Light green	368	240	1310
	Very dark brown*	839	891	2208
▲	Medium gold	676	891	2208 ⎱

used together with one strand of Balger blending filament in gold ⎰

Note: use very dark brown* to outline the bow, and dark red* for the background lines (both shades are used for bks only).

CHRISTMAS BORDER ▶		DMC	ANCHOR	MADEIRA
P	Dark salmon	760	9	0405
	Light pink red*	3328	11	0406
●	Dark red	347	19	0407
X	Apple green	320	216	1311
S	Dark green	319	246	1405
▲	Very dark brown	839	380	1913
L	Medium gold	676	891	2208 ⎱

used together with one strand of Balger blending filament in gold ⎰

Note: use light pink red* (used for bks only) to outline the hearts, and one strand of medium gold with one strand of gold blending

CHRISTMAS WELCOME ▶		DMC	ANCHOR	MADEIRA
O	Light pink red	3328	11	0406
●	Dark red	347	19	0407
X	Apple green	320	216	1311
S	Dark green	319	246	1405
B	Medium beige brown	841	378	1911
╲	Light beige brown	842	378	1910
·	White	White	1	White
	Very dark brown*	839	380	1913
C	Medium gold	676	891	2208 ⎱

used together with one strand of Balger blending filament in gold ⎰

Note: use very dark brown* (used for bks only) to outline the door.

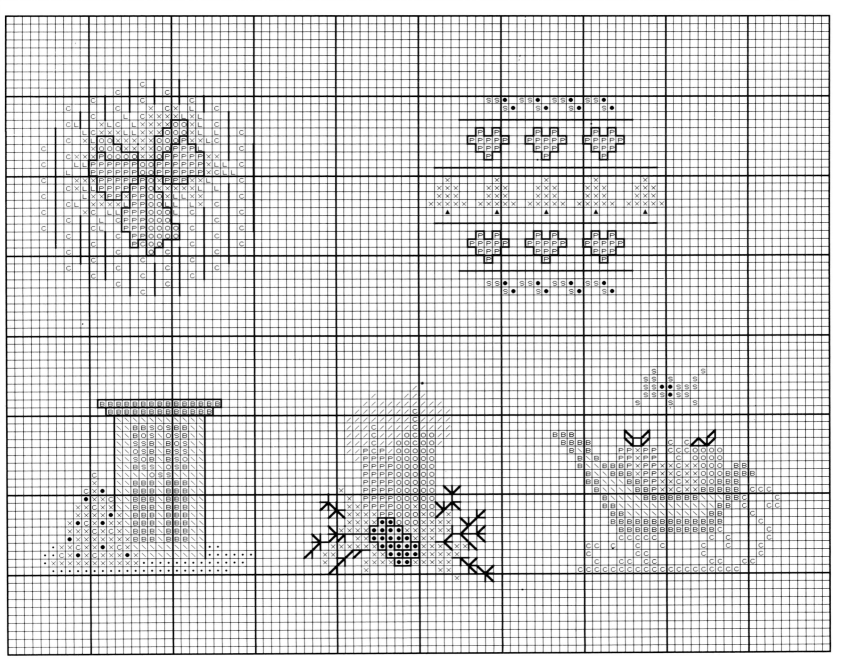

CHRISTMAS LIGHTS ▲	DMC	ANCHOR	MADEIRA
P Dark salmon	760	9	0405
O Light pink red	3328	11	0406
● Dark red	347	19	0407
X Apple green	320	216	1311
Dark green*	319	246	1405
╱ Light gold			
(half cross stitch only)	677	886	2205
Very dark brown*	839	380	1913
C Medium gold	676	891	2208 ⎫

used together with one strand of Balger blending filament in gold ⎰

Note: outline the holly berries in very dark brown* and backstitch the fir branches in dark green* (both used for bks only).

SLEIGH ▲	DMC	ANCHOR	MADEIRA
P Dark salmon	760	9	0405
O Light pink red	3328	11	0406
● Dark red	347	19	0407
X Apple green	320	216	1311
Dark green*	319	246	1405
B Medium beige brown	841	378	1911
╲ Light beige brown	842	376	1910
C Medium gold	676	891	2208 ⎫

used together with one strand of Balger blending filament in gold ⎰

Festive Table Linen

A set of hand-embroidered Christmas table linen, complete in every detail – even individual placecards – will delight your family and guests, and set the scene for one of the happiest days of the year.

FESTIVE TABLE LINEN

YOU WILL NEED

For the set of six plastic Napkin Holders,
Placecards and Placements, and the single Table
Runner (sizes given below):

Six napkin holders
15cm × 7cm (6in × 3in) of white, 22-count
Hardanger fabric (sufficient for six napkin holders)
15cm × 7cm (6in × 3in) of ultra-soft,
medium-weight, iron-on interfacing, to back the
napkin holders
Six red placecards, with 2.3cm (⁷⁄₈in) circular
cut-outs
15cm × 10cm (6in × 4in) of white, 18-count Aida
fabric (sufficient for six placecards)
15cm × 10cm (6in × 4in) of ultra-soft, medium-
weight, iron-on interfacing, to back the placecards
Six 40.6cm (16in) square dinner napkins
Six 33cm × 48.5cm (13in × 19in) placemats
33cm × 96.5cm (13in × 38in) table runner
Stranded embroidery cotton in the colours given
in the panel
No26 tapestry needle

NOTE The napkin holders, placecards, napkins,
placemats and runner are all obtainable from
specialist suppliers, see page 220.

●

NAPKIN HOLDERS

Using rows of basting stitches, divide the Hardanger fabric into six equal sections. Take the holly
design from the Christmas bows border, and
embroider one holly motif at the centre of each
section, using two strands of embroidery cotton in
the needle throughout.

Press the finished embroidery. Iron the interfacing to the back of the fabric, then cut along the
basted lines to separate the six holders. For each
holder, trim the fabric to measure 4.3cm × 3.8cm
(1⅝in × 1½in), and place the embroidery inside
the clear plastic holder.

PLACECARDS

Using rows of basting stitches, divide the Aida
fabric into six equal sections. Take the holly
design from the Christmas bows border, and
embroider one motif at the centre of each section,
using two strands of embroidery cotton in the
needle throughout.

Press the finished embroidery. Iron the interfacing to the back of the fabric, then cut along the
basted lines to separate the six holders. For each
placecard, trim the fabric to measure 4cm (1½in)
square.

Position your design behind the round aperture.
When you are happy that it is correctly centred,
use a small piece of clear tape to hold it while you
seal the card. Remove the backing strip from the
panel on the left of the placecard; fold it over, and
press firmly to seal the two halves of the placecard
together. You can then add the names or wording
you require, perhaps using a gold or silver pen.

TABLE LINEN

All of the designs are stitched over two threads of
the 26-count fabric used for these ready-prepared
table linens, and two strands of embroidery cotton
are used in the needle throughout.

The dinner napkins feature the Christmas bows
border, which runs along the side edges, 2.5cm
(1in) in from the fringe.

For the placemats, embroider the holly border,
again placing it along the side edges, 2.5cm (1in)
in from the fringe.

For the table runner, start by marking the centre
with two lines of basting stitches (see page 9).
Stitch the holly wreath at the centre of the runner,
then measure out for 25.5cm (10in) on each side of
the central vertical line. Stitch the holly border at
this point on each side of the runner.

When you have completed the holly borders,
embroider a Christmas bows border down each
side, 2.5cm (1in) out from the holly border, and the
same distance in from the fringed edge.

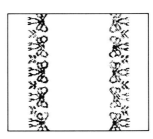

Napkin

Placemat

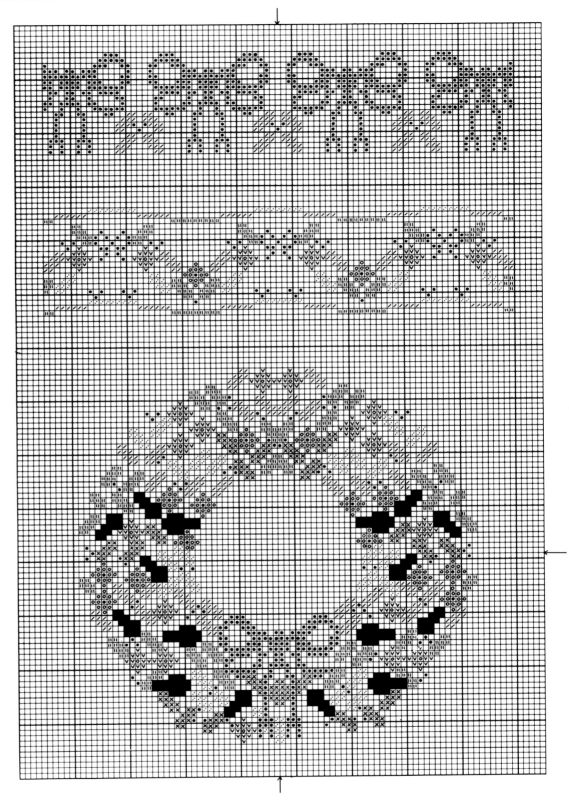

Table Runner

TABLE LINEN ▲	DMC	ANCHOR	MADEIRA
● Bright orange red	606	335	0209
⦁ Bright Christmas green	704	256	1308
╱ Kelly green	702	226	1306
‖ Christmas green	699	923	1303
∨ Bright canary yellow	973	297	0105
◯ Medium tangerine orange	941	304	0203
✕ Light loden green	3364	843	1603
■ Khaki	370	888	2112

205

Cake Band and Glass Coasters

Complement your cake with this pretty cake band, which you can keep and re-use for years to come. A set of glass coasters with snowflake motifs provides the perfect finishing touch to your Christmas table.

CAKE BAND AND GLASS COASTERS

SNOWFLAKES ▶	DMC	ANCHOR	MADEIRA
White	White	2	White

YOU WILL NEED

For the Cake Band, measuring 85cm × 10cm (33½in × 4in):

87.5cm (34½in) of green Aida band, 10cm (4in) deep, with silver edging
Silver thread
No24 tapestry needle
Sewing thread to match the Aida

For a set of six Coasters, each 7cm (2¾in) in diameter:

27cm × 18cm (10¾in × 7in) of navy, 18-count Aida fabric
27cm × 18cm (10¾in × 7in) of ultra-soft, medium-weight, iron-on interfacing
Stranded embroidery cotton as given in the appropriate panel
No26 tapestry needle
Six glass coasters (for suppliers, see page 220)

•

CAKE BAND

Use silver metallic thread and centre the design along the Aida band, remembering to leave 12mm (½in) clear at each end for the seam allowances. Embroider the cross stitch design; there are 14 pattern repeats.

When you have finished the embroidery, turn under a double 6mm (¼in) hem at each short end. Attach the band to the cake either with pins or with small blobs of icing.

GLASS COASTERS

Divide the Aida fabric with lines of basting stitches into six equal sections. Set the fabric in a hoop or frame and complete the cross stitch embroidery, using two strands of embroidery cotton in the needle throughout, and ensuring that each design is centred within a section, When you have finished, remove basting stitches, and press.

Iron the interfacing to the wrong side of your fabric. This will prevent fraying, and will also enable you to see the pencil lines made when you draw around the paper templates provided with the coasters. You may, however, find it easier to use a pair of compasses to draw a 6cm (2¼in) circle on the interfacing around each design (make sure that they are centred within their circles).

For each coaster, cut a fabric circle and place it in the recess on the base of a coaster. Put a paper template on the reverse side of the embroidery, then peel the backing from the protective base and carefully place it over the back of the coaster, ensuring that the embroidery and template remain in position.

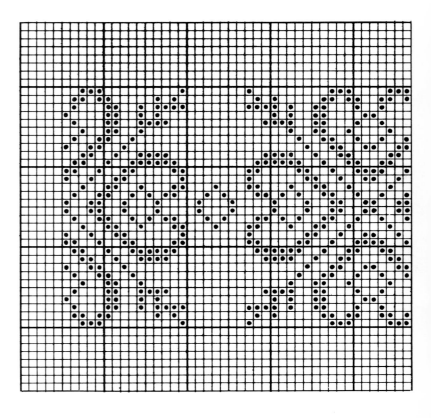

CAKE BAND ▶
Silver thread

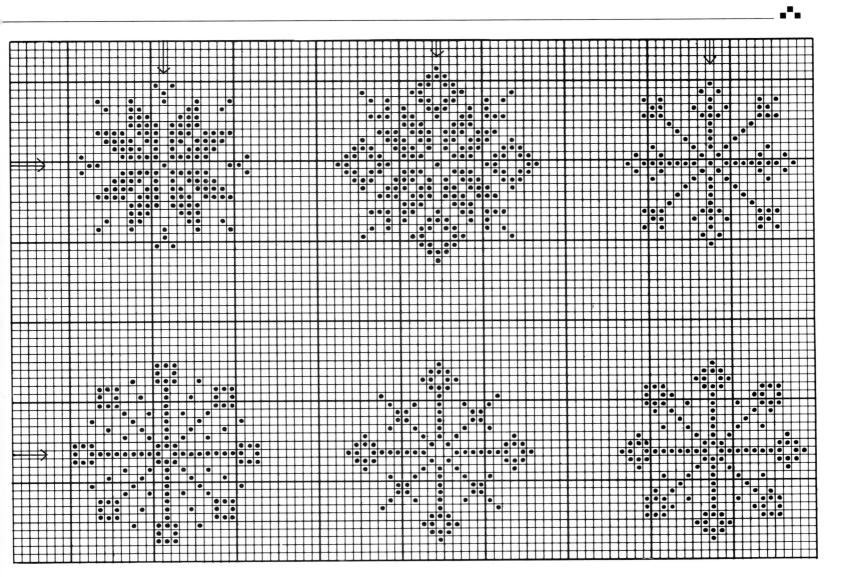

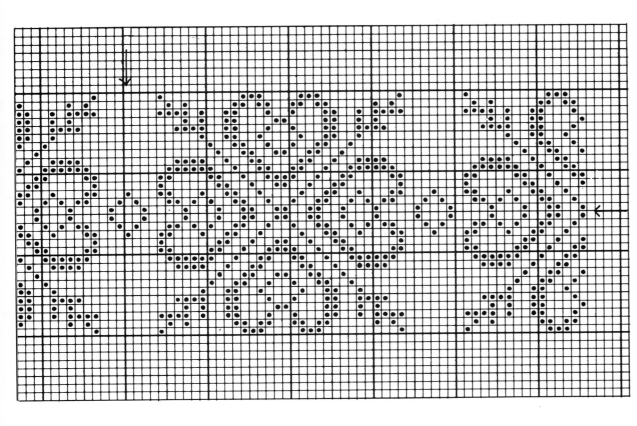

Christmas Crackers

These pretty Christmas crackers offer a novel way of wrapping gifts. Each cracker can be filled with sweets, jewellery or other small gifts.

CHRISTMAS CRACKERS

YOU WILL NEED

For each Cracker, measuring 22.5cm (9in) long and 4cm (1⅝in) in diameter:

28cm × 19cm (11in × 7½in) of white, holly green or Christmas red, 14-count Aida fabric
112cm (44in) of red or green ribbon, 6mm (¼in) wide
Stranded embroidery cotton in the colours given in the appropriate panel
Gold metallic thread
No24 tapestry needle
Cardboard tube from the centre of a toilet roll
Double-sided tape

•

THE EMBROIDERY

Prepare the fabric, marking the centre with basting stitches, and stretch it in a hoop (see page 9). Using two strands of embroidery cotton in the needle throughout, complete your chosen design. Remove basting stitches and press the finished embroidery, pressing a 12mm (½in) seam allowance to the wrong side down each long edge.

MAKING THE CRACKER

Fray the two short edges for 2.5cm (1in), removing the cross threads of the Aida one at a time.

Place the embroidery face down on a firm, flat surface. Put a strip of double-sided tape along the complete length of one of the pressed seam allowances (on the wrong side of the embroidery).

Put another strip of double-sided tape along the length of the cardboard tube. Lay the taped tube against the seam allowance. Make sure that the tube is centred, so that an equal amount of fabric extends beyond the tube at each end.

Carefully roll the fabric around the tube, pressing the taped seam allowance firmly where the fabric meets.

Cut the ribbon into two equal lengths; take one length and tie it in a bow around one end of the cracker. Place your gift inside the cardboard tube, and tie the remaining length of ribbon into a bow around the other end of the cracker, which is now ready to be hung on the tree.

ROBIN ▶		DMC	ANCHOR	MADEIRA
II	Very light topaz yellow	727	293	0110
∕	Light emerald green	912	209	1212
●	Light red	350	11	0213
■	Black	310	403	Black
∴	Medium cocoa brown	407	882	2310
C	Chocolate	632	936	2311
◢	Dark beige brown	839	905	1913

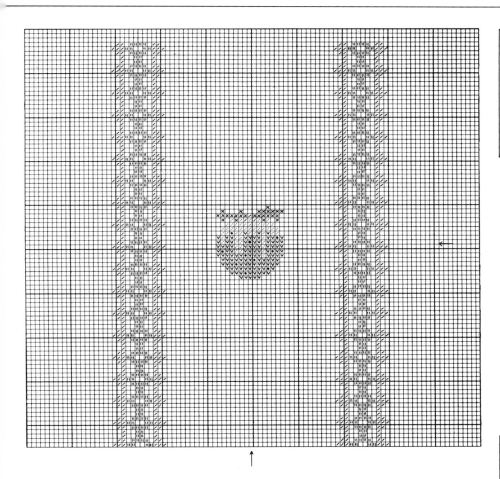

PUDDING ◄		DMC	ANCHOR	MADEIRA
⟋	Red	349	13	0212
‖	Gold thread	—	—	—
⊠	Light chartreuse green	704	256	1308
⊡	White	White	2	White
⊽	Tan brown	436	363	2011
⬤	Dark coffee brown	801	357	2007

WREATH ▼		DMC	ANCHOR	MADEIRA
◺	Chartreuse	703	238	1307
⊠	Red	349	13	0212
⊡	White	White	2	White

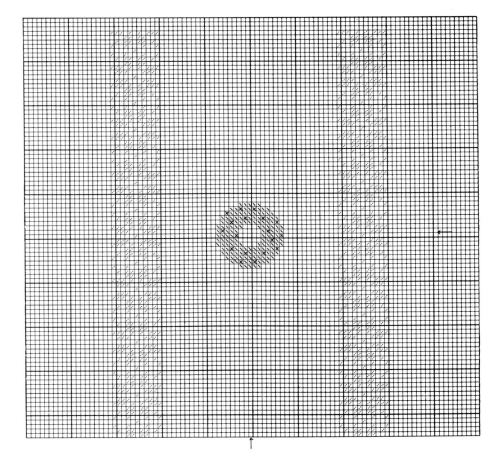

Christmas Stocking

This lovely embroidered stocking is just the right size to hold small sweets and toys, or a small teddy. It is a present which will delight any child at Christmas.

CHRISTMAS STOCKING

YOU WILL NEED

For the Christmas Stocking, measuring approximately 31cm × 28cm (12½in × 11¼in):

Two 38cm × 30.5cm (15in × 12in) pieces of holly green, 14-count Aida fabric
1.5m (1⅔yds) of red bias binding, 12mm (½in) wide
Stranded embroidery cotton in the colours given in the panel
No 24 tapestry needle
Red sewing thread

●

THE EMBROIDERY

Take one of the two pieces of Aida fabric; prepare it for embroidery and set it in a hoop or frame (see page 9). Embroider the design; work the cross stitch first, using two strands of embroidery cotton in the needle, and then the backstitch, using one strand.

Gently press the finished embroidery on the wrong side, using a steam iron.

MAKING THE STOCKING

Trace the stocking template on good quality tracing paper, marking the position of the arrows. Centre this over the embroidery; mark and then cut out the shape. Reversing the tracing paper pattern, cut a mirror-image shape from the remaining piece of Aida.

Place the two pieces with wrong sides together and baste around the edge. Machine stitch, taking a 12mm (½in) seam allowance and leaving the top open. Trim the edge to within 6m (¼in) of the stitching line and remove basting stitches.

Pin and baste the red bias binding all around the stitched edge and around the open top edge of the stocking. Stitching through all layers, stitch the binding in position. If you intend to hang the stocking, make a small hanging loop from a short length of the binding and stitch this to the top of the stocking, at the back seam.

Each square measures 2.5cm (1in)

STOCKING ▶		DMC	ANCHOR	MADEIRA
☑	Bright Christmas red	666	46	0210
C	Medium garnet red	815	43	0513
⦂	White	White	2	White
☒	Topaz yellow	725	306	0108
●	Black	310	403	Black
‖	Medium steel grey	317	400	1714
・	Light peach	754	6	0305
∧	Medium peach	352	9	0303
H	Medium Delft blue	799	130	0910
∨	Royal blue	797	132	0912
I	Golden wheat	3046	887	2206
O	Dark golden wheat	3045	888	2103
≡	Medium violet	553	98	0712
L	Light Chartreuse green	704	256	1308
Z	Very light golden yellow	3078	292	0102

Note: bks white with medium steel grey; light peach with medium peach and golden wheat with dark golden wheat.

INDEX

ACKNOWLEDGEMENTS

The author and publishers would like to thank
the following for their help in supplying fabric, threads
and products for use in many of the projects in the book:

DMC Creative World Ltd and Framecraft Miniatures Ltd.
Both suppliers request that a stamped self-addressed
envelope be enclosed with all enquiries.

SUPPLIERS

*The following mail order
companies have supplied
some of the basic items
needed for making up the
projects in this book:*

Framecraft Miniatures Limited
372/376 Summer Lane
Hockley
Birmingham, B19 3QA
England
Telephone: (0121) 359 4442

Sew It All
Garden Cottage
Oving
Buckinghamshire
Telephone: (01296) 641524

*Addresses for Framecraft
stockists worldwide*

Ireland Needlecraft Pty Ltd
2-4 Keppel Drive
Hallam, Victoria 3803
Australia

Danish Art Needlework
PO Box 442, Lethbridge
Alberta T1J 3Z1
Canada

Sanyei Imports
PO Box 5, Hashima Shi
Gifu 501-62
Japan

The Embroidery Shop
286 Queen Street
Masterton
New Zealand

Anne Brinkley Designs Inc.
246 Walnut Street
Newton
Mass. 02160
USA

S A Threads and Cottons Ltd.
43 Somerset Road
Cape Town
South Africa

*For information on your nearest
stockist of embroidery cotton,
contact the following:*

DMC
*(also distributors of
Zweigart fabrics)*

UK
DMC Creative World Limited
62 Pullman Road
Wigston
Leicester, LE8 2DY
Telephone: 0116 811040

USA
The DMC Corporation
Port Kearney Bld.
10 South Kearney
N.J. 07032-0650
Telephone: 201 589 0606

AUSTRALIA
DMC Needlecraft Pty
P.O. Box 317
Earlswood 2206
NSW 2204
Telephone: 02599 3088

COATS AND ANCHOR

UK
McMullen Road
Darlington
Co. Durham DL1 1YQ
Telephone: 01325 381010

USA
Coats & Clark
P.O. Box 27067
Dept CO1
Greenville SC 29616
Telephone: 803 234 0103

AUSTRALIA
Coats Patons Crafts
Thistle Steet
Launceston
Tasmania 7250
Telephone: 00344 4222

MADEIRA

UK
Madeira Threads (UK) Limited
Thirsk Industrial Park
York Road, Thirsk
N. Yorkshire, YO7 3BX
Telephone: 01845 524880

USA
Madeira Marketing Limited
600 East 9th Street
Michigan City
IN 46360
Telephone: 219 873 1000

AUSTRALIA
Penguin Threads Pty Limited
25-27 Izett Street
Prahran
Victoria 3181
Telephone: 03529 4400